Translucent Stained Glass
Coloring Book

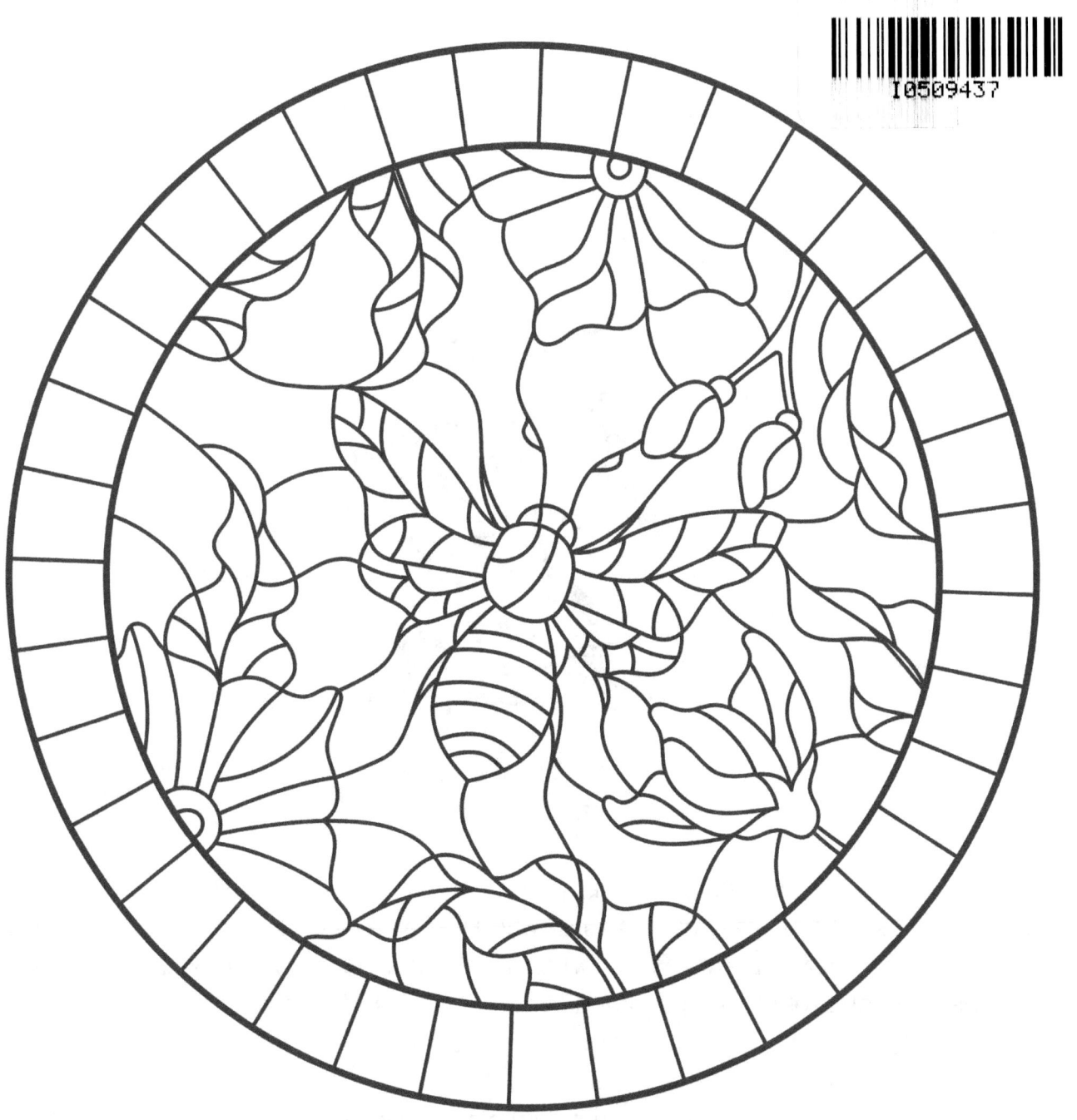

An Adults Coloring Book

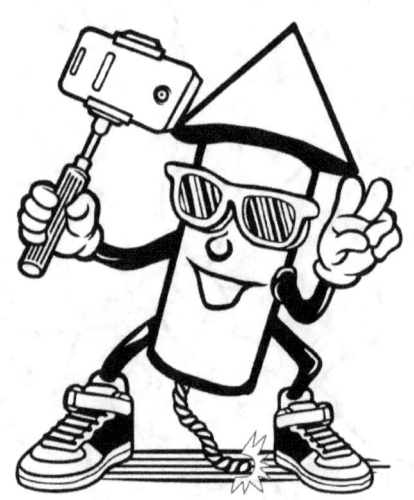

PUBLISHED IN 2020 BY
FIREWORK PUBLISHING

COPYRIGHT 'ILLUSTRATIONS' 2020 FIREWORK PUBLISHING
ALL RIGHT RESERVED.'NO PART OF THIS PUBLICATION MAY BE REPRODUCED OR TRANSMITTED IN ANY
FORM OR BY ANY MEANS, ELECTRONIC OR MECHANICAL, INCLUDING PHOTOCOPY RECORDING OR ANY
INFORMATION STORAGE SYSTEM AND RETRIEVAL SYSTEM WITHOUT PERMISSION IN WRITING
BY FIREWORK PUBLISHING

PRINTED IN THE UNITED STATE OF AMERICA

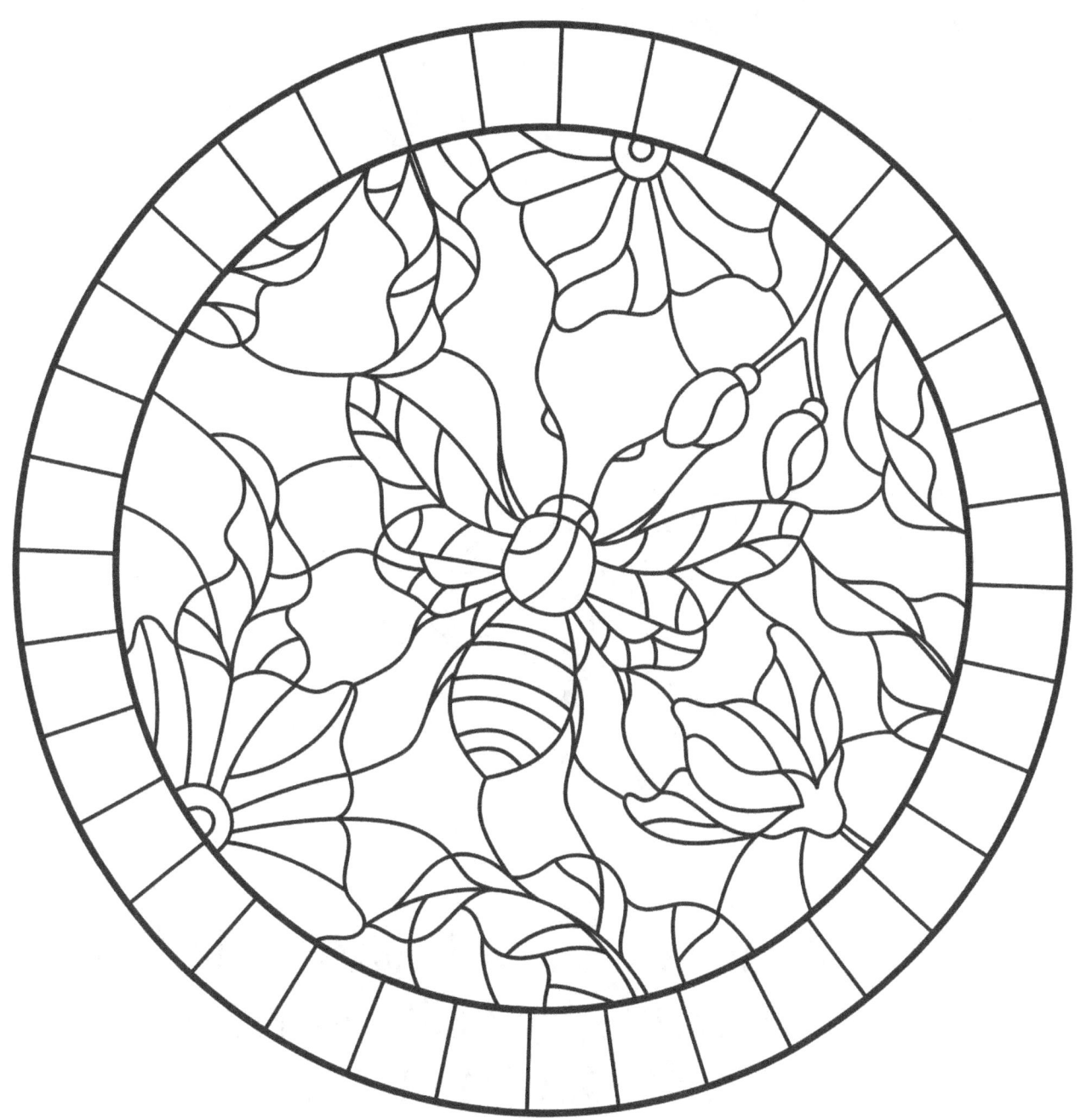

This book belongs to
_____

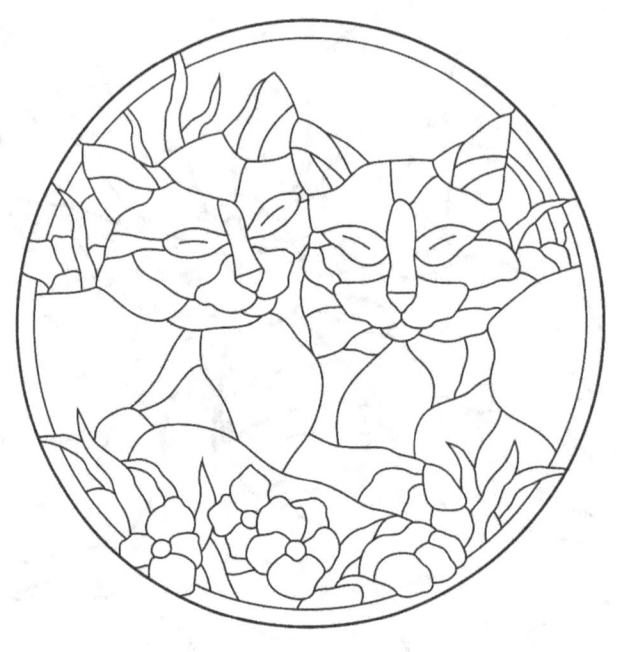

"For me a stained glass window
is a transparent partition
between my heart
and the heart of the world"

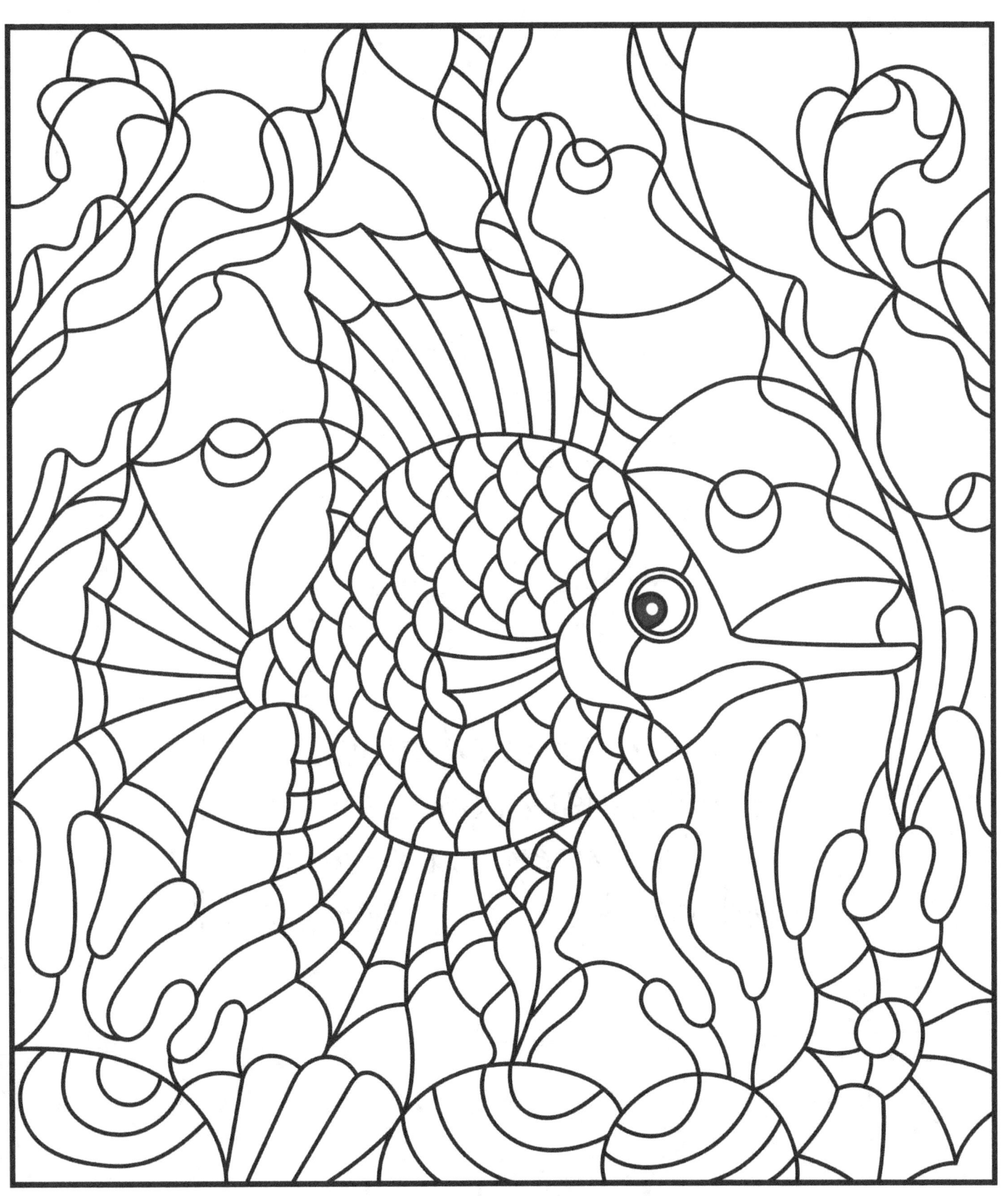

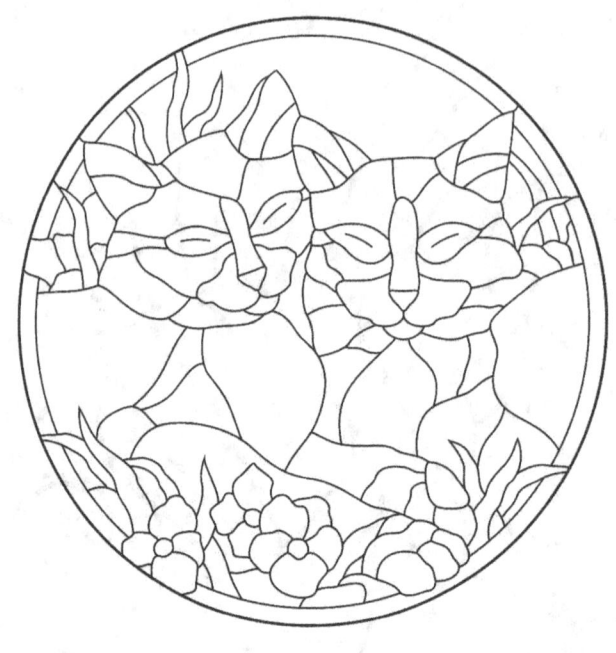

"For me a stained glass window
is a transparent partition
between my heart
and the heart of the world"

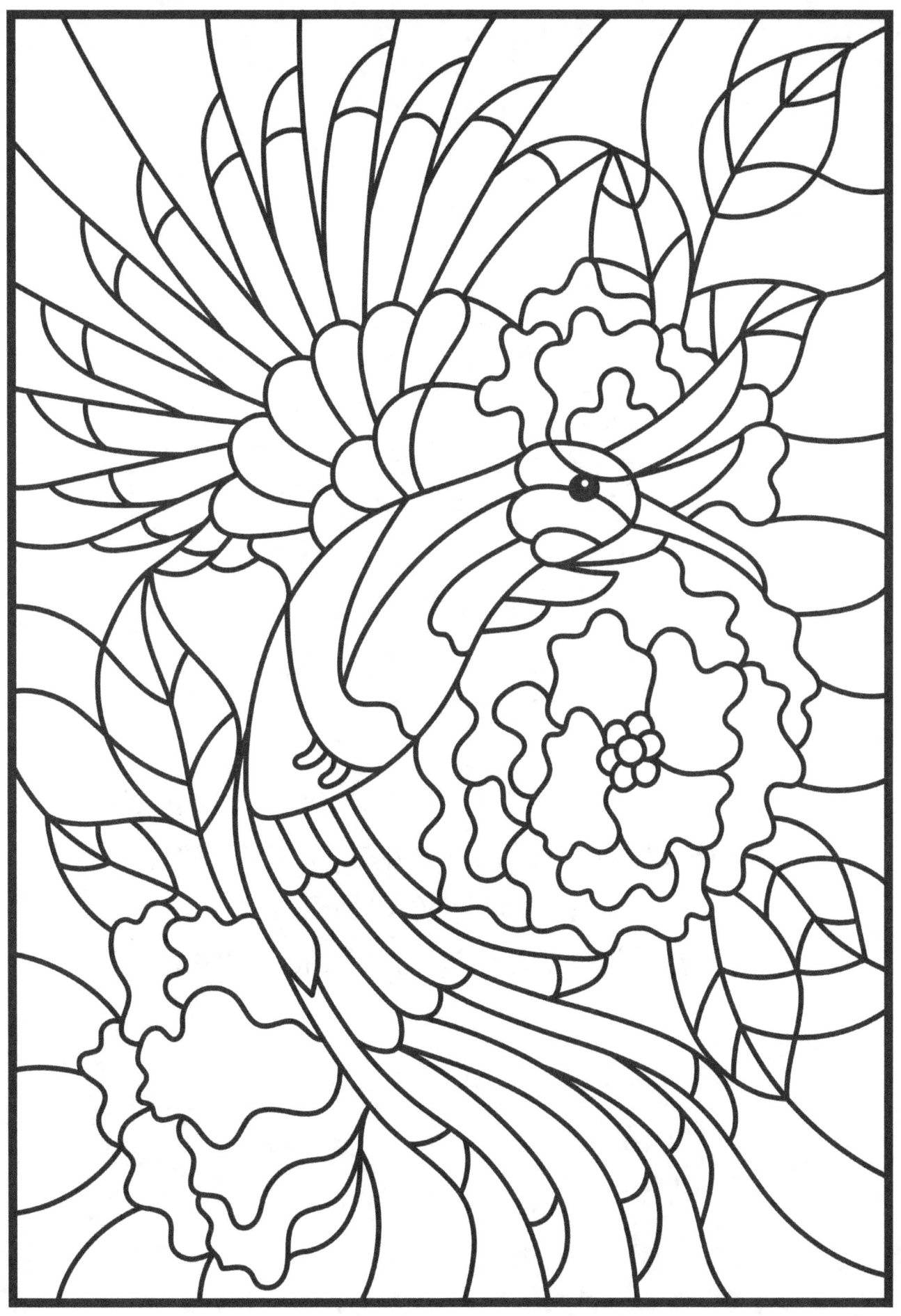

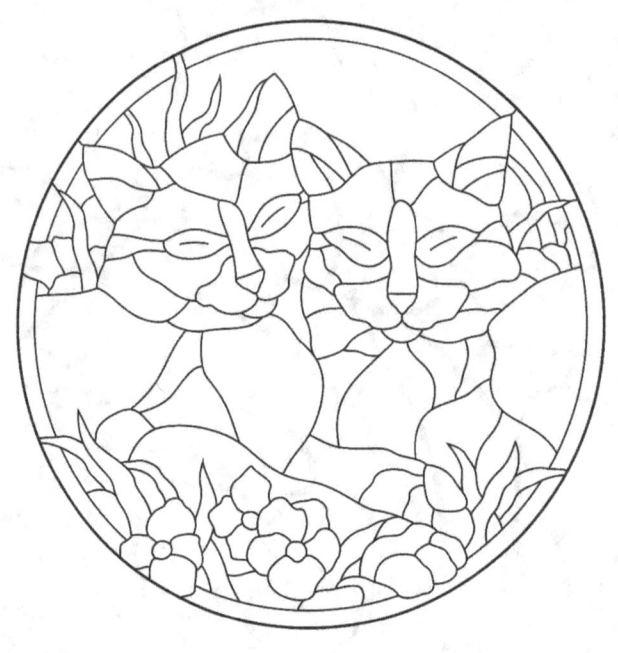

"For me a stained glass window
is a transparent partition
between my heart
and the heart of the world"

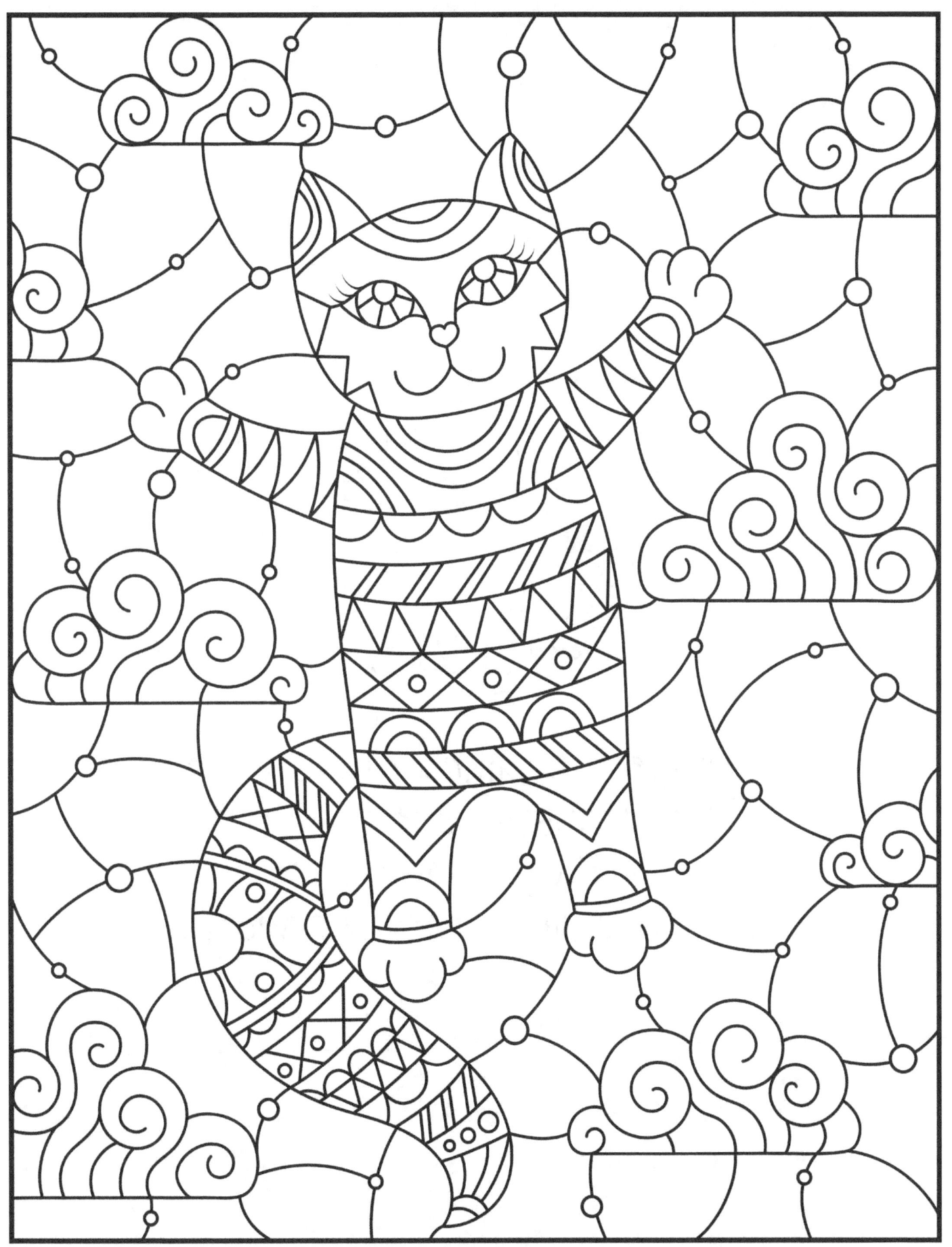

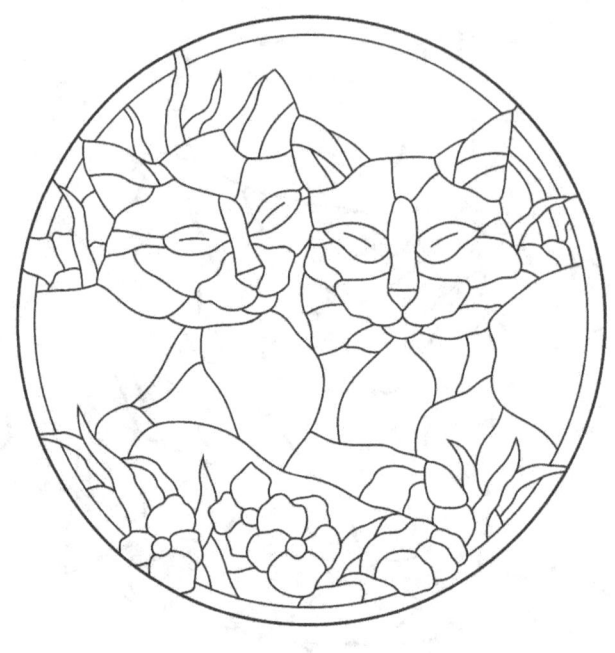

"For me a stained glass window
is a transparent partition
between my heart
and the heart of the world"

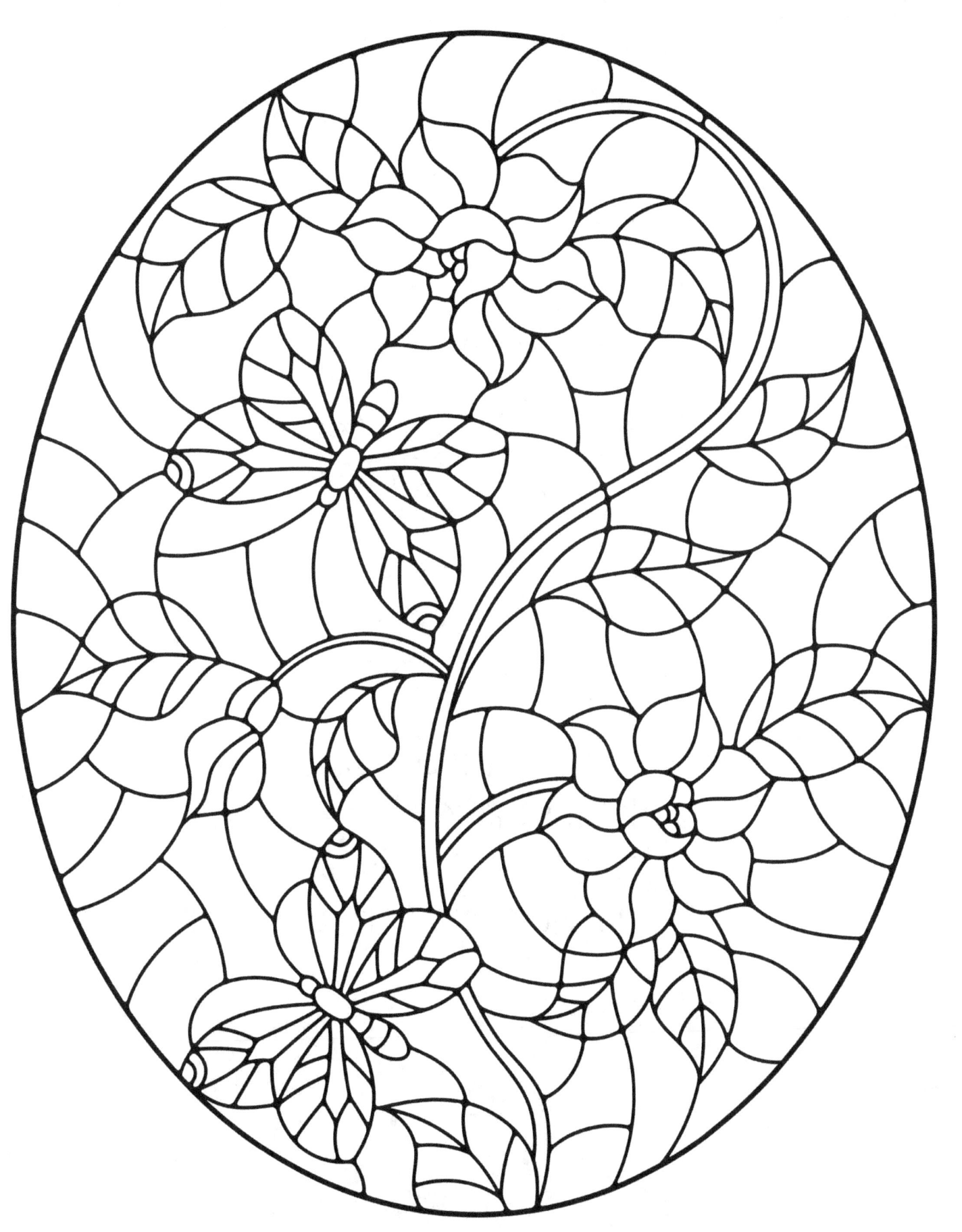

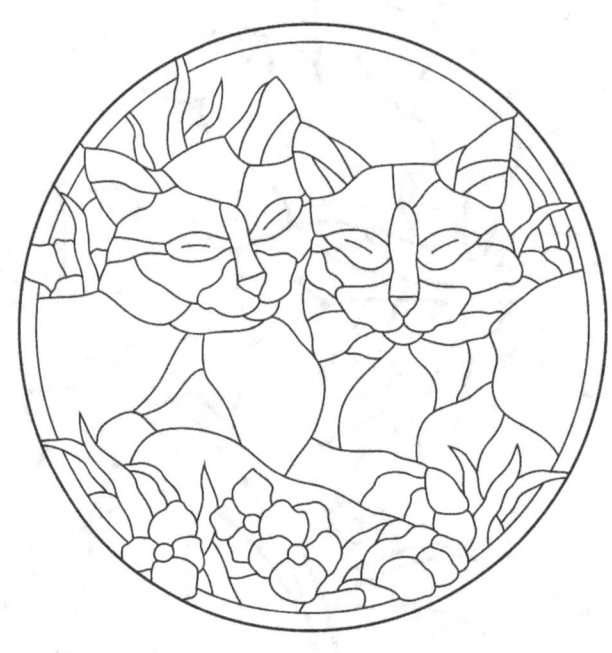

"For me a stained glass window
is a transparent partition
between my heart
and the heart of the world"

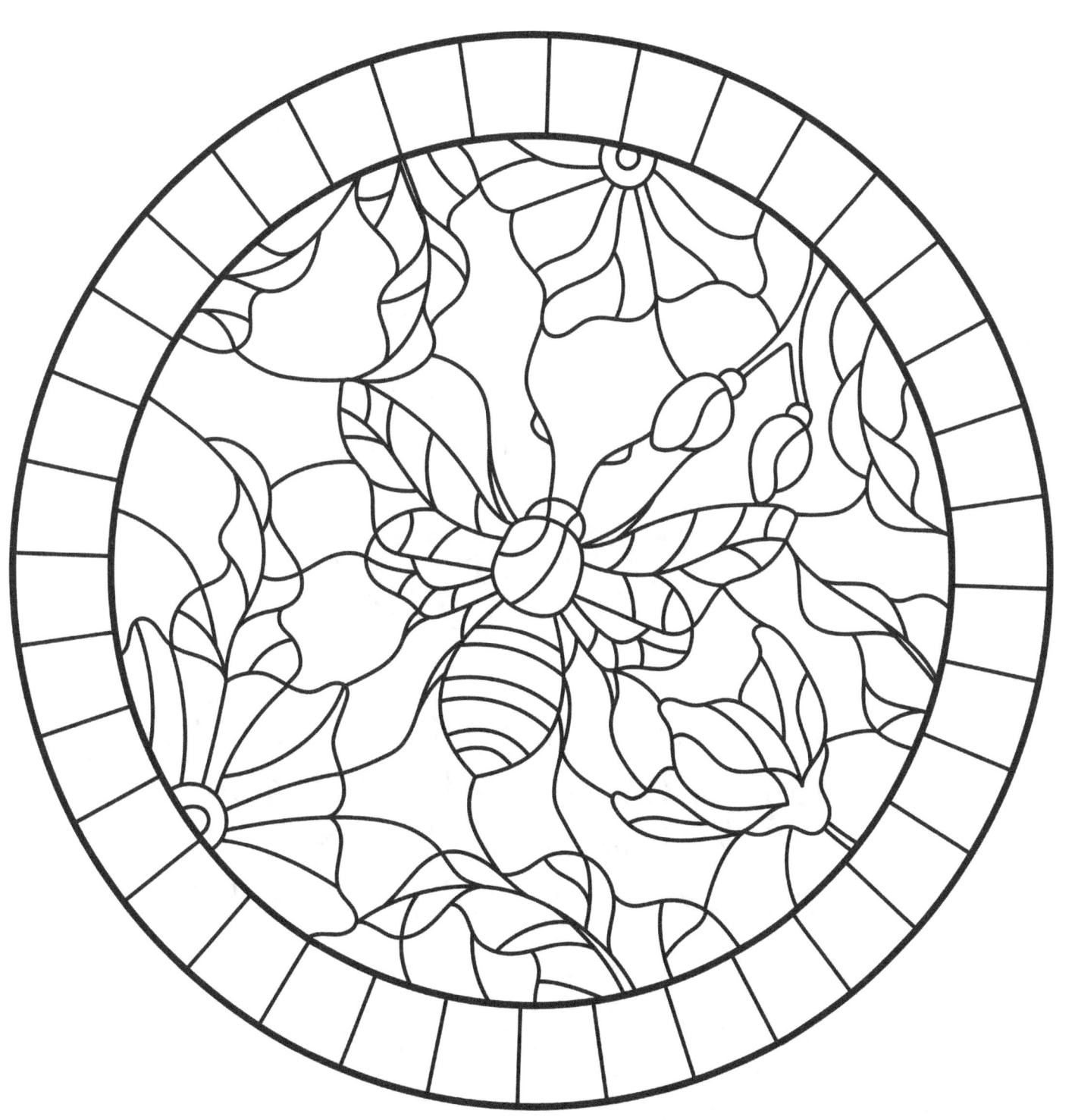

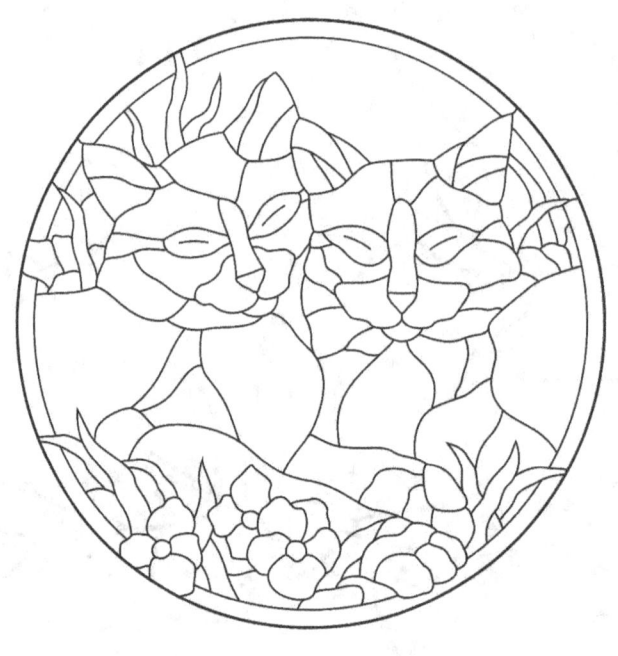

"For me a stained glass window
is a transparent partition
between my heart
and the heart of the world"

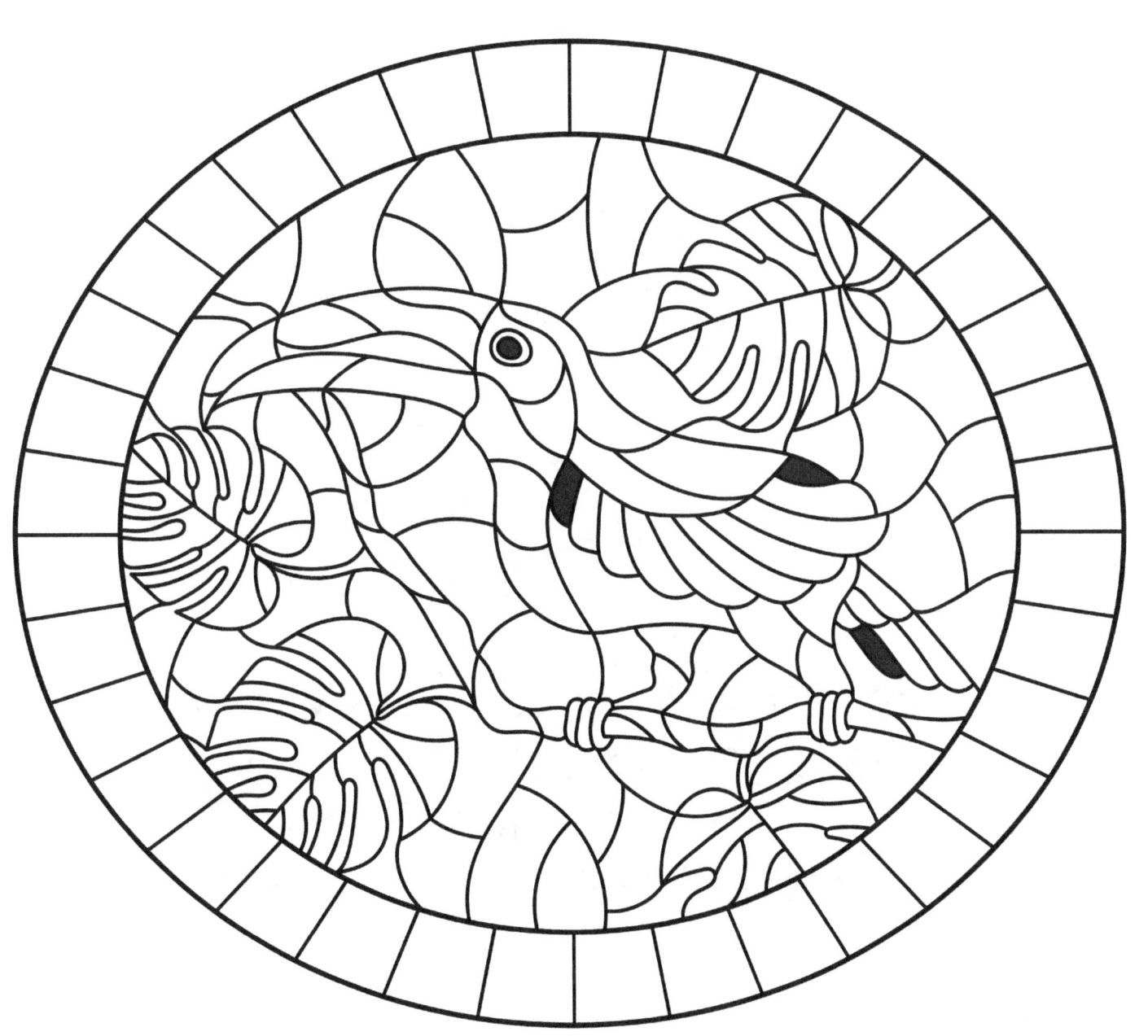

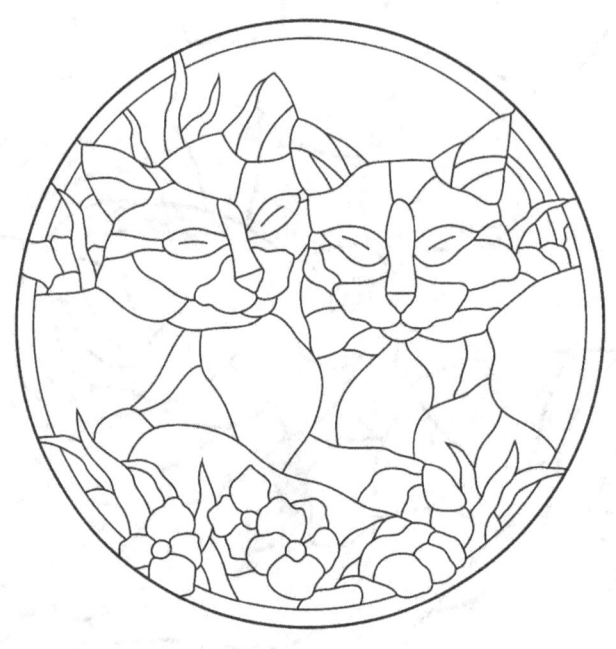

"For me a stained glass window
is a transparent partition
between my heart
and the heart of the world"

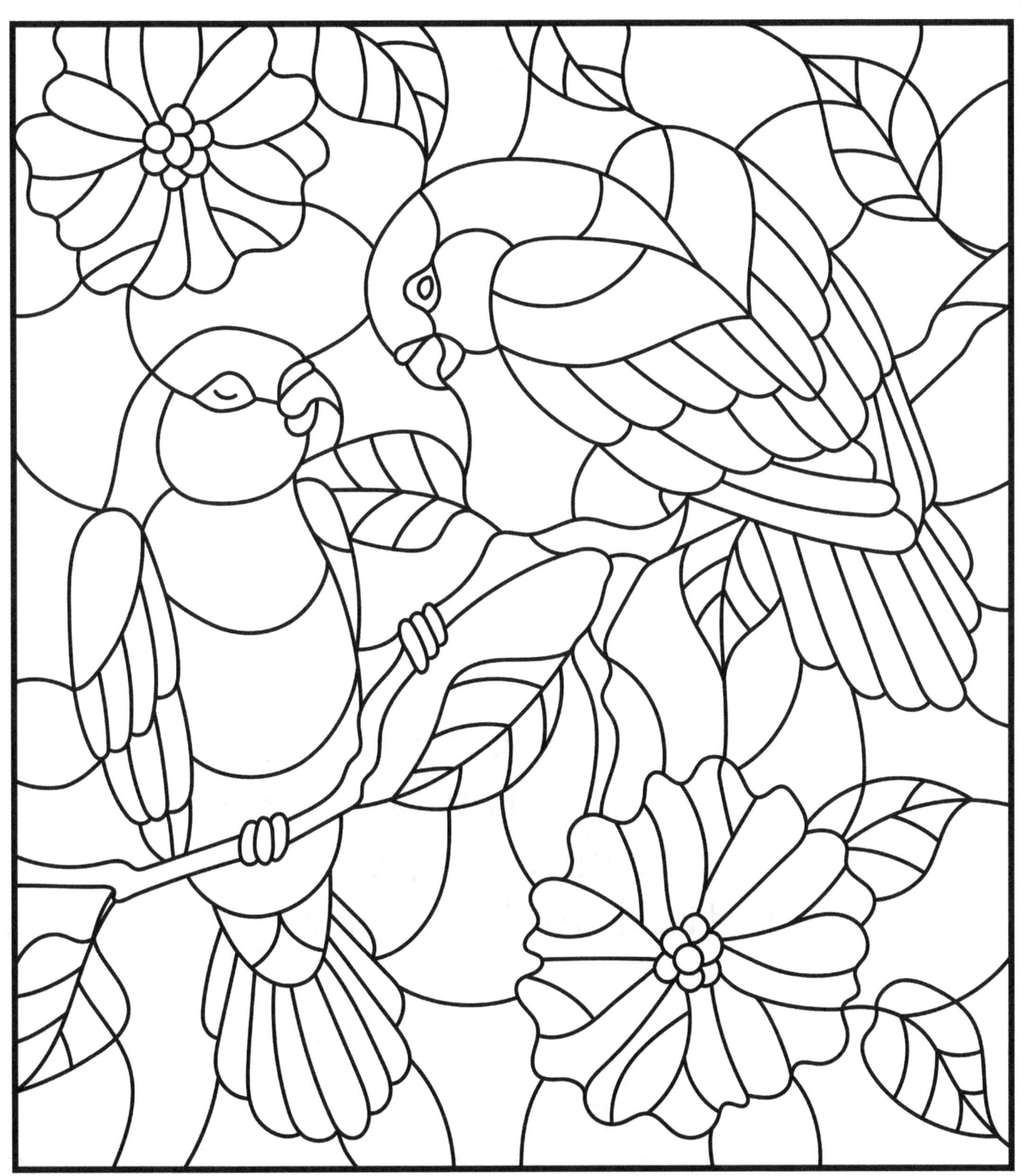

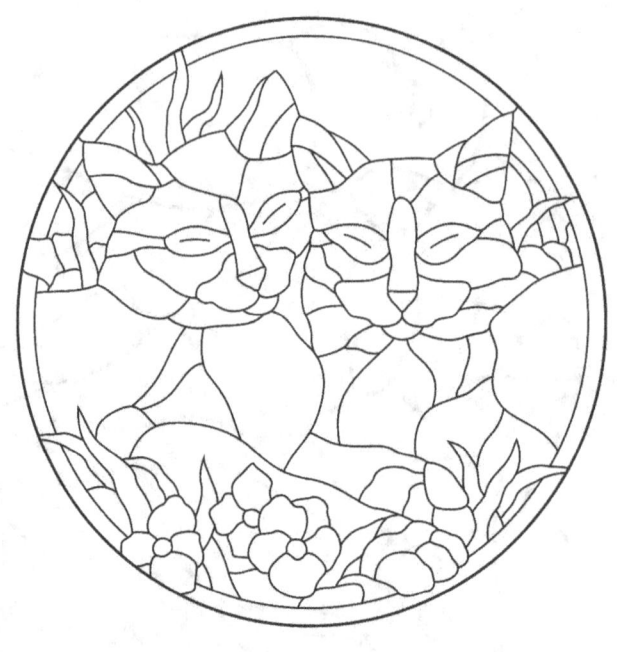

"For me a stained glass window
is a transparent partition
between my heart
and the heart of the world"

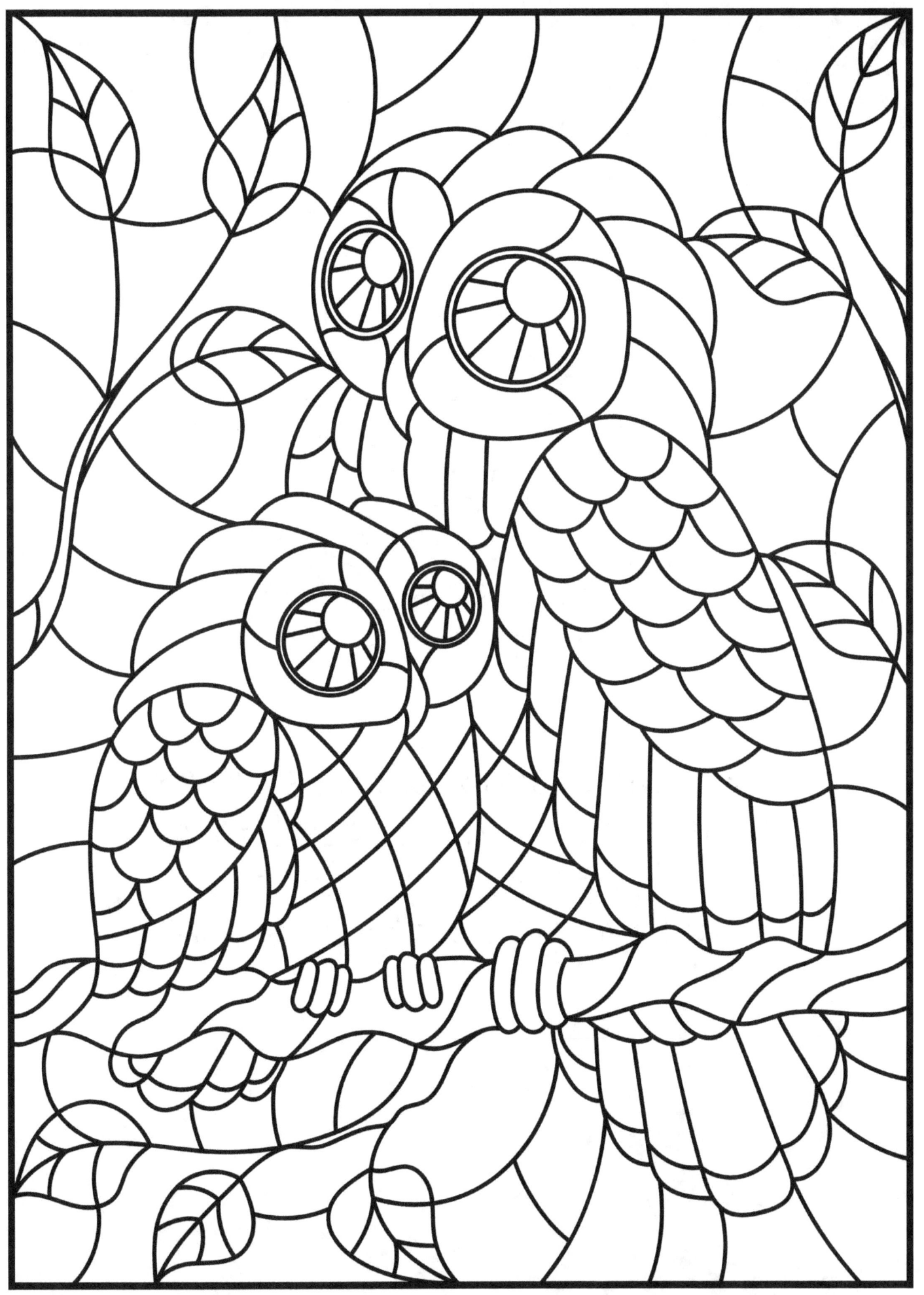

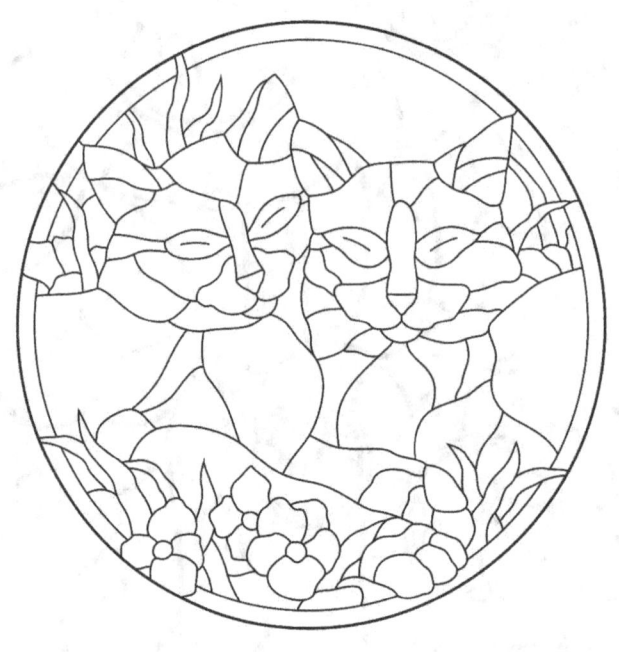

"For me a stained glass window
is a transparent partition
between my heart
and the heart of the world"

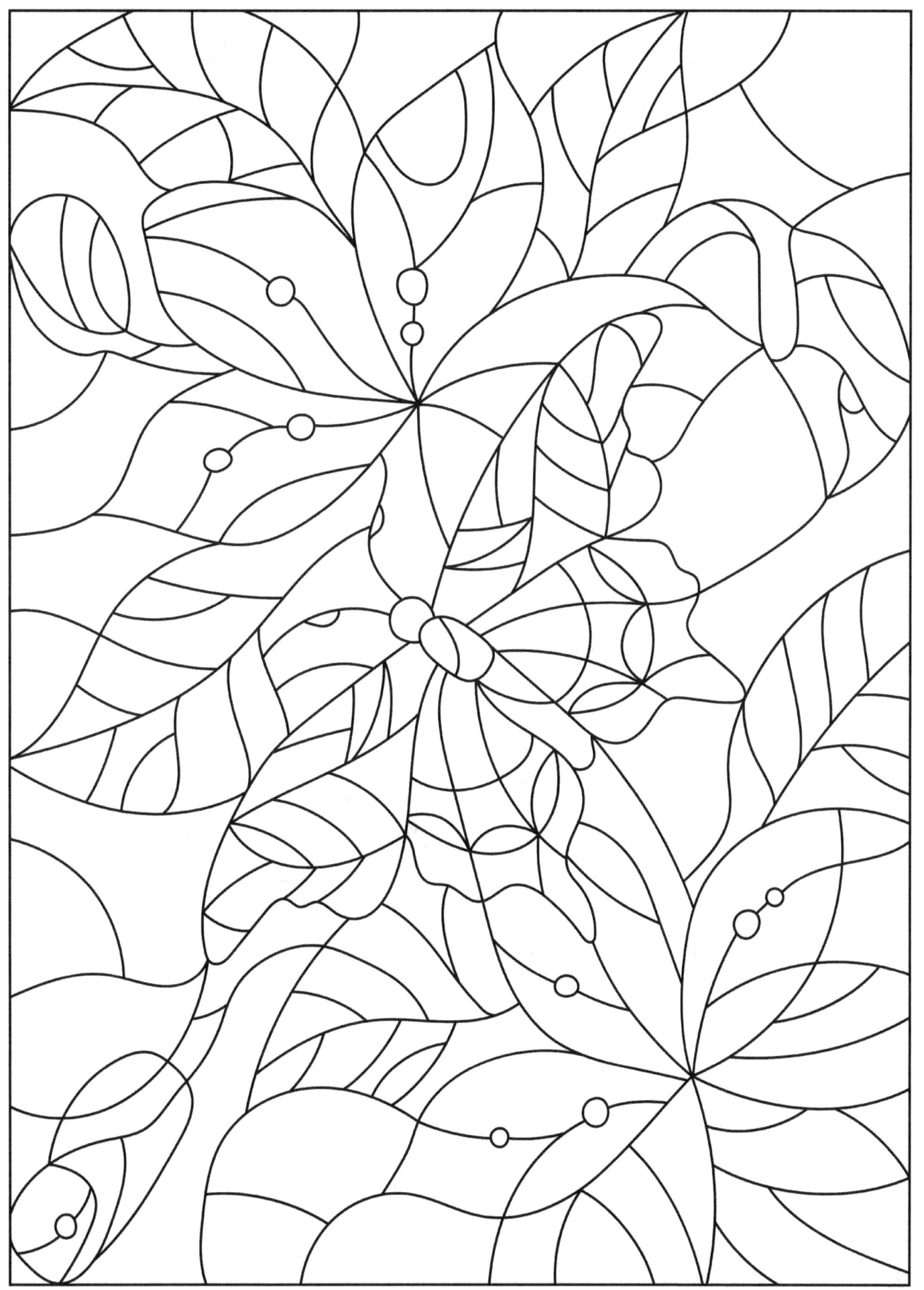

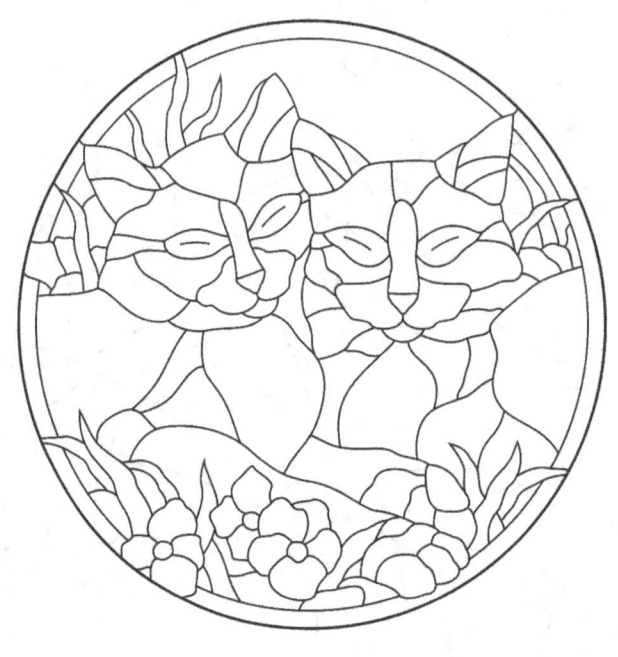

"For me a stained glass window
is a transparent partition
between my heart
and the heart of the world"

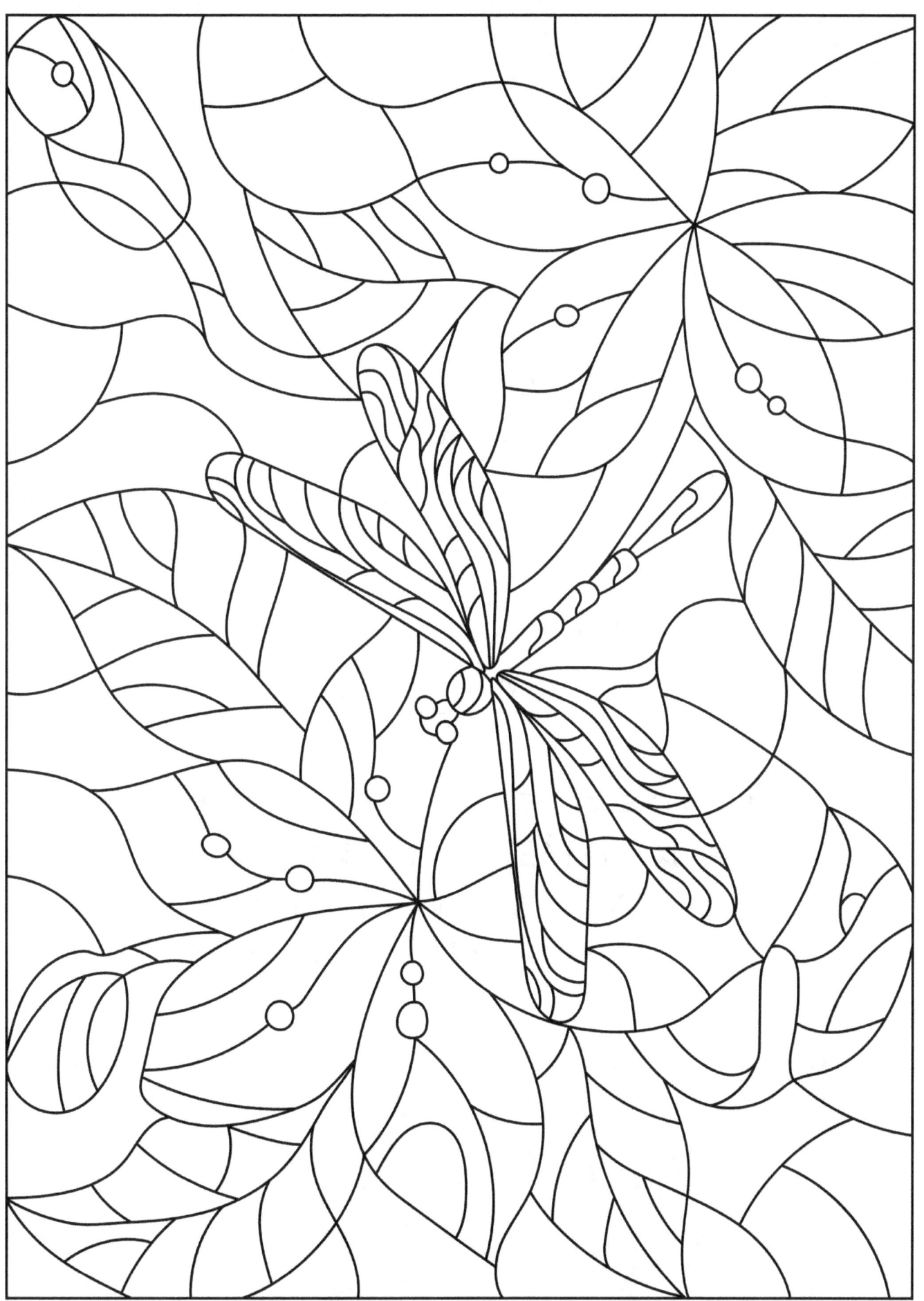

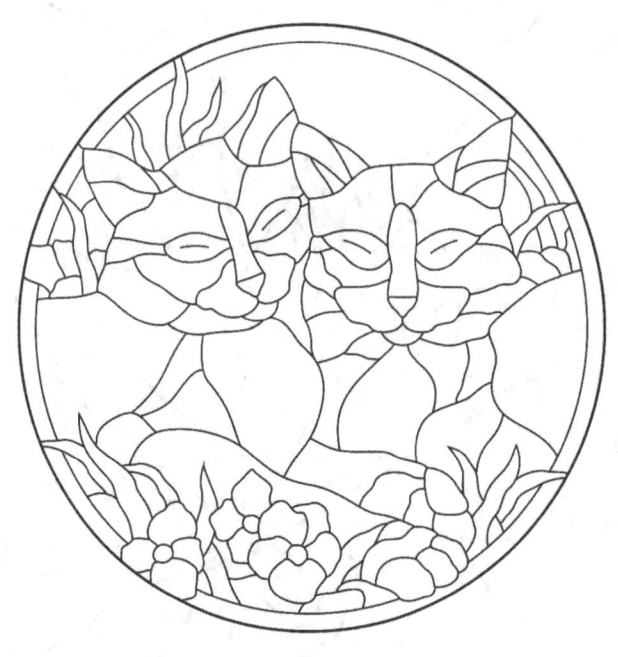

"For me a stained glass window
is a transparent partition
between my heart
and the heart of the world"

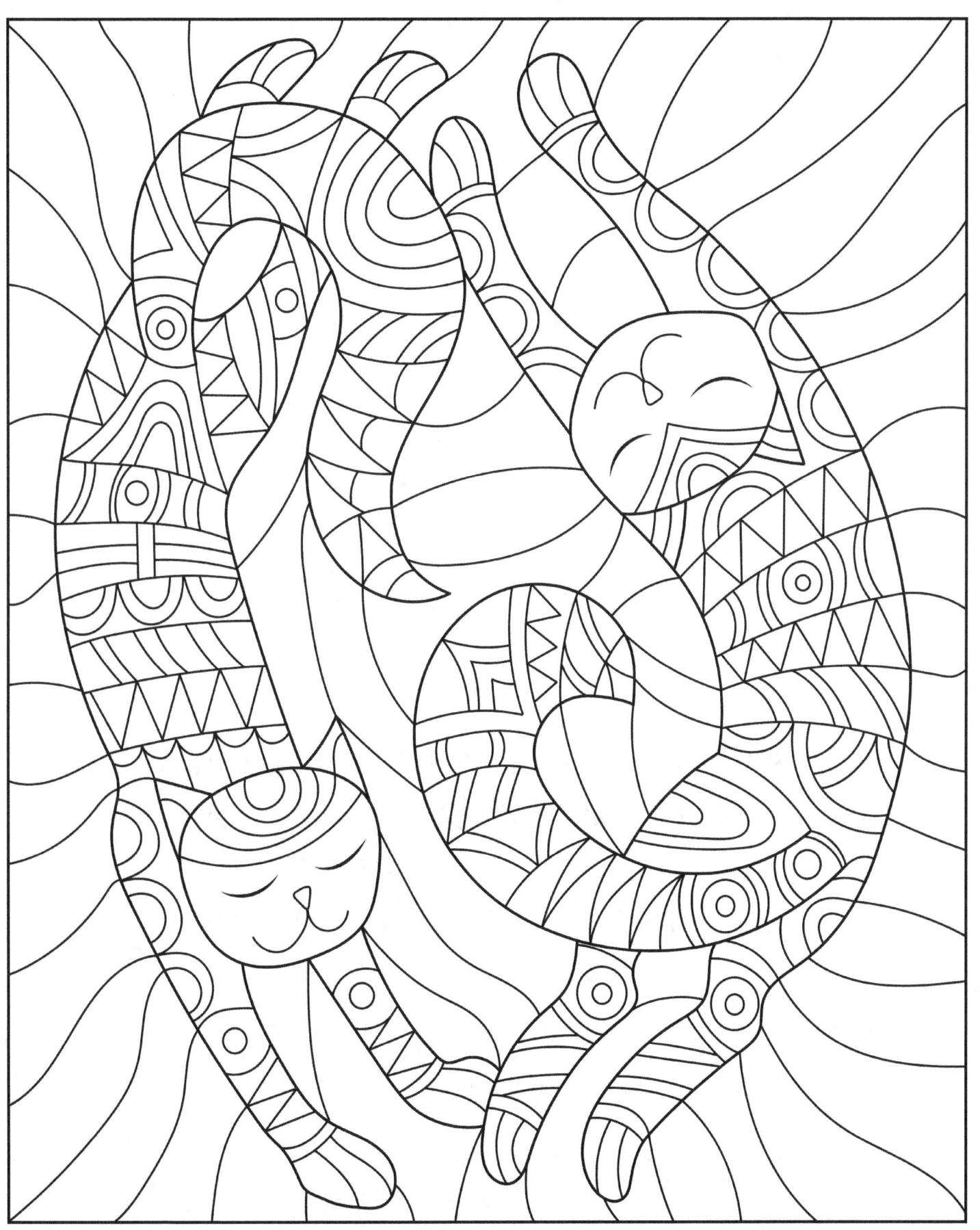

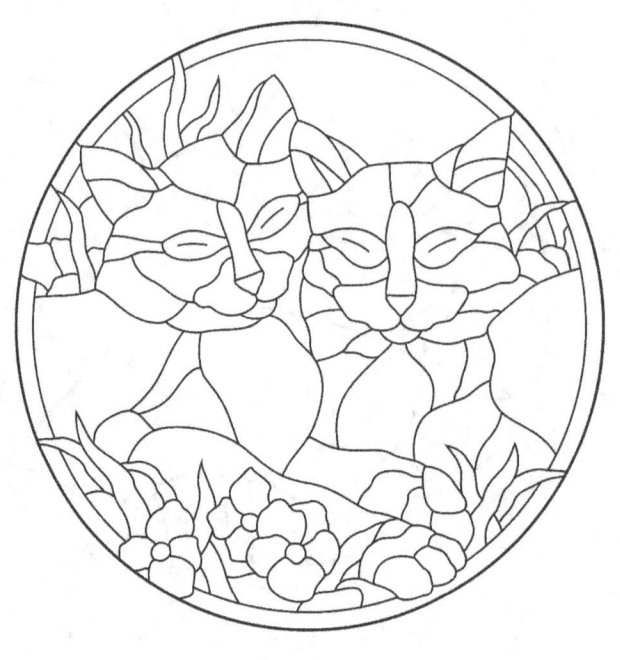

"For me a stained glass window
is a transparent partition
between my heart
and the heart of the world"

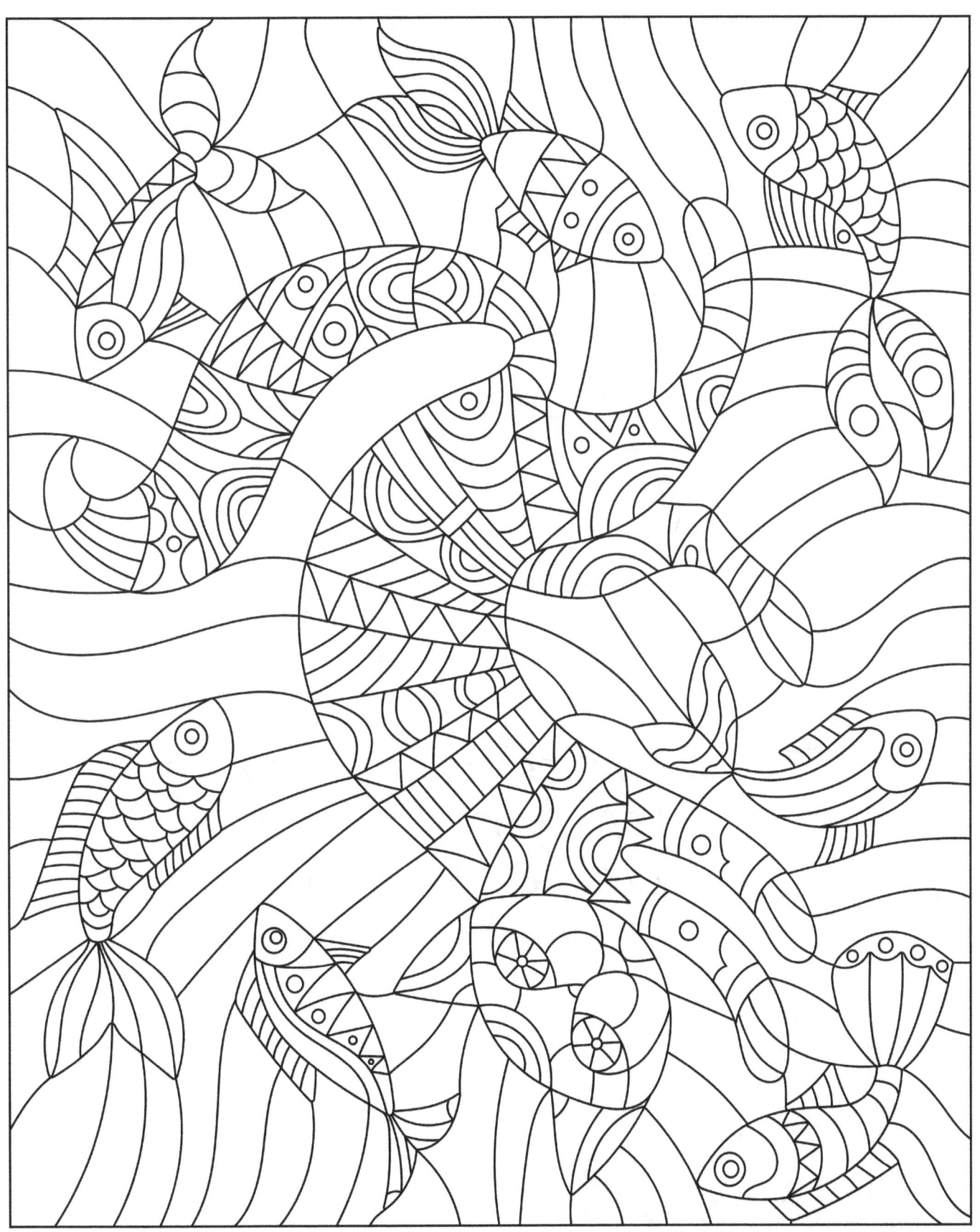

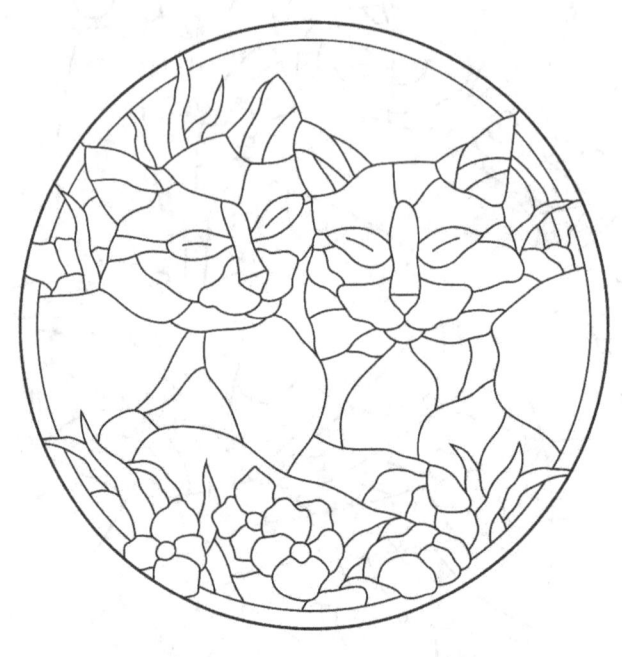

"For me a stained glass window
is a transparent partition
between my heart
and the heart of the world"

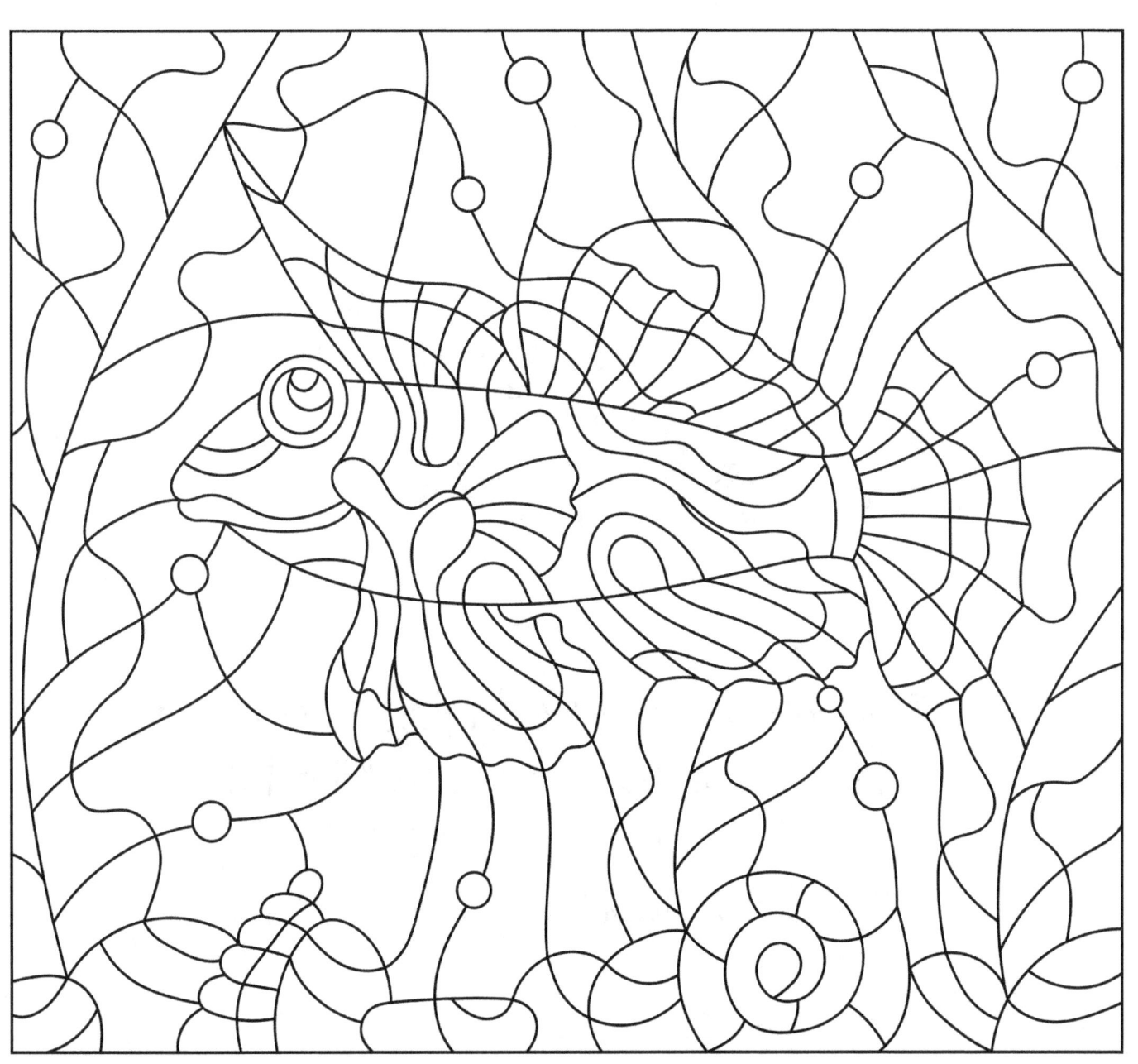

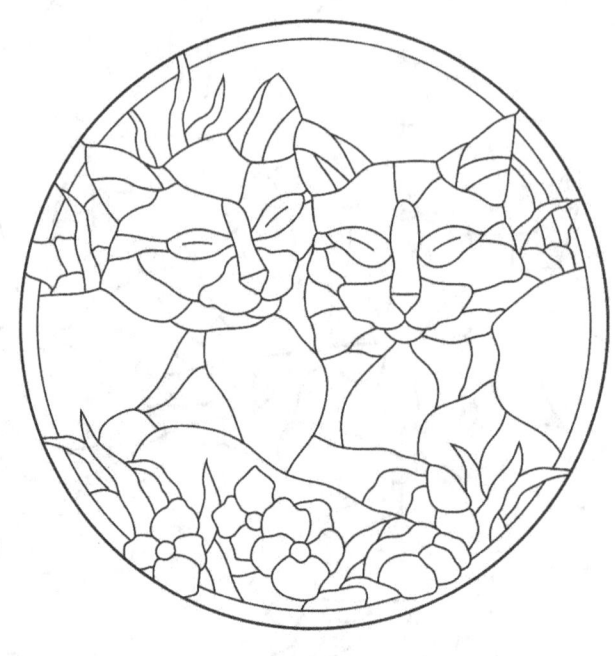

"For me a stained glass window
is a transparent partition
between my heart
and the heart of the world"

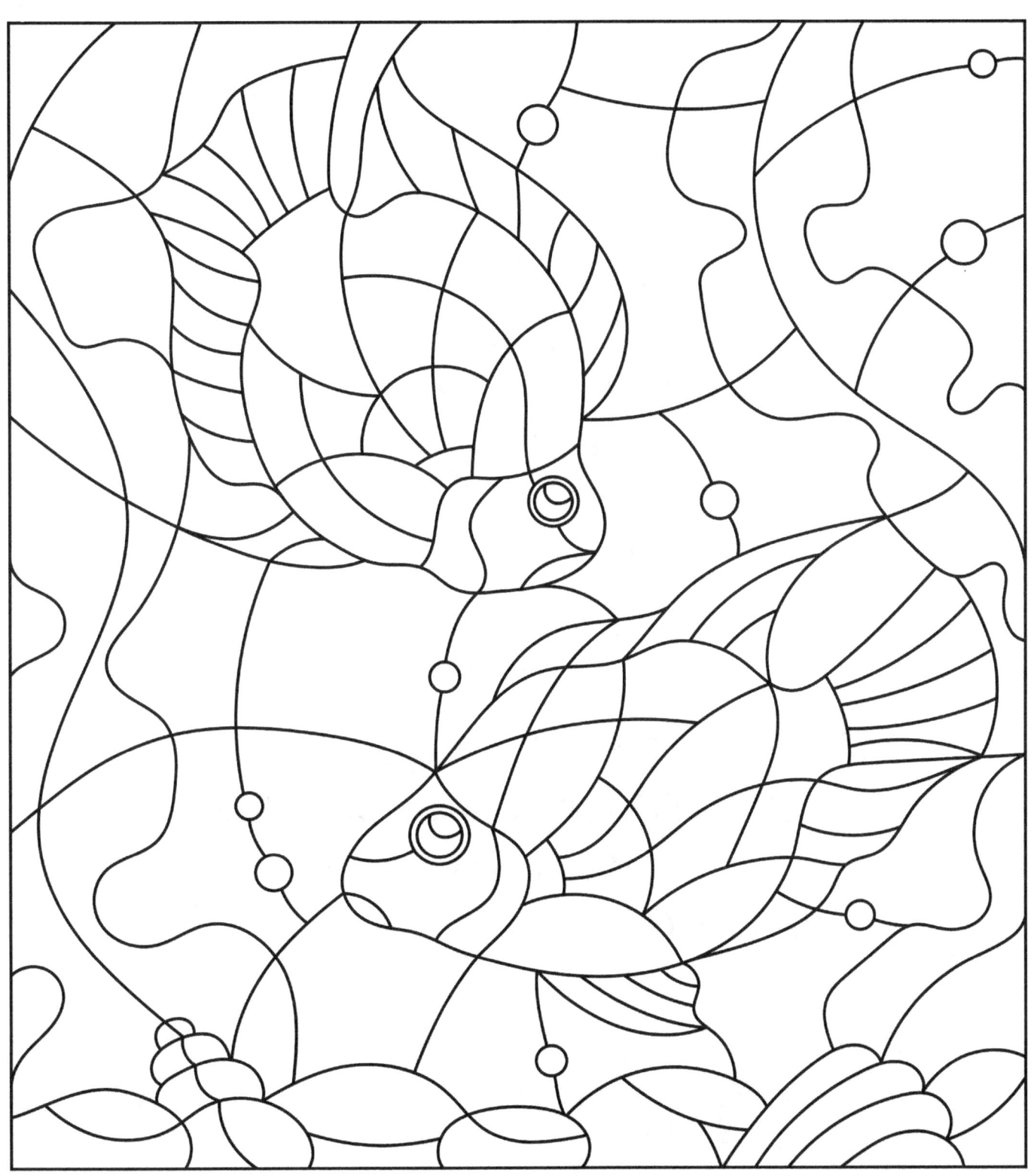

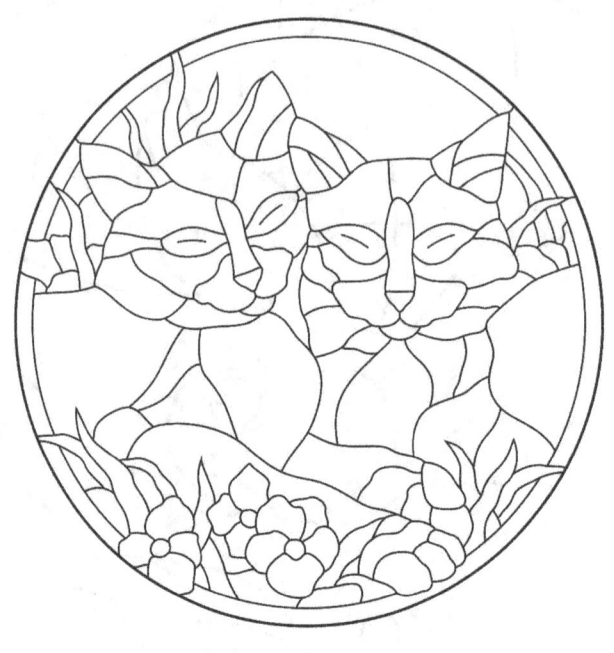

"For me a stained glass window
is a transparent partition
between my heart
and the heart of the world"

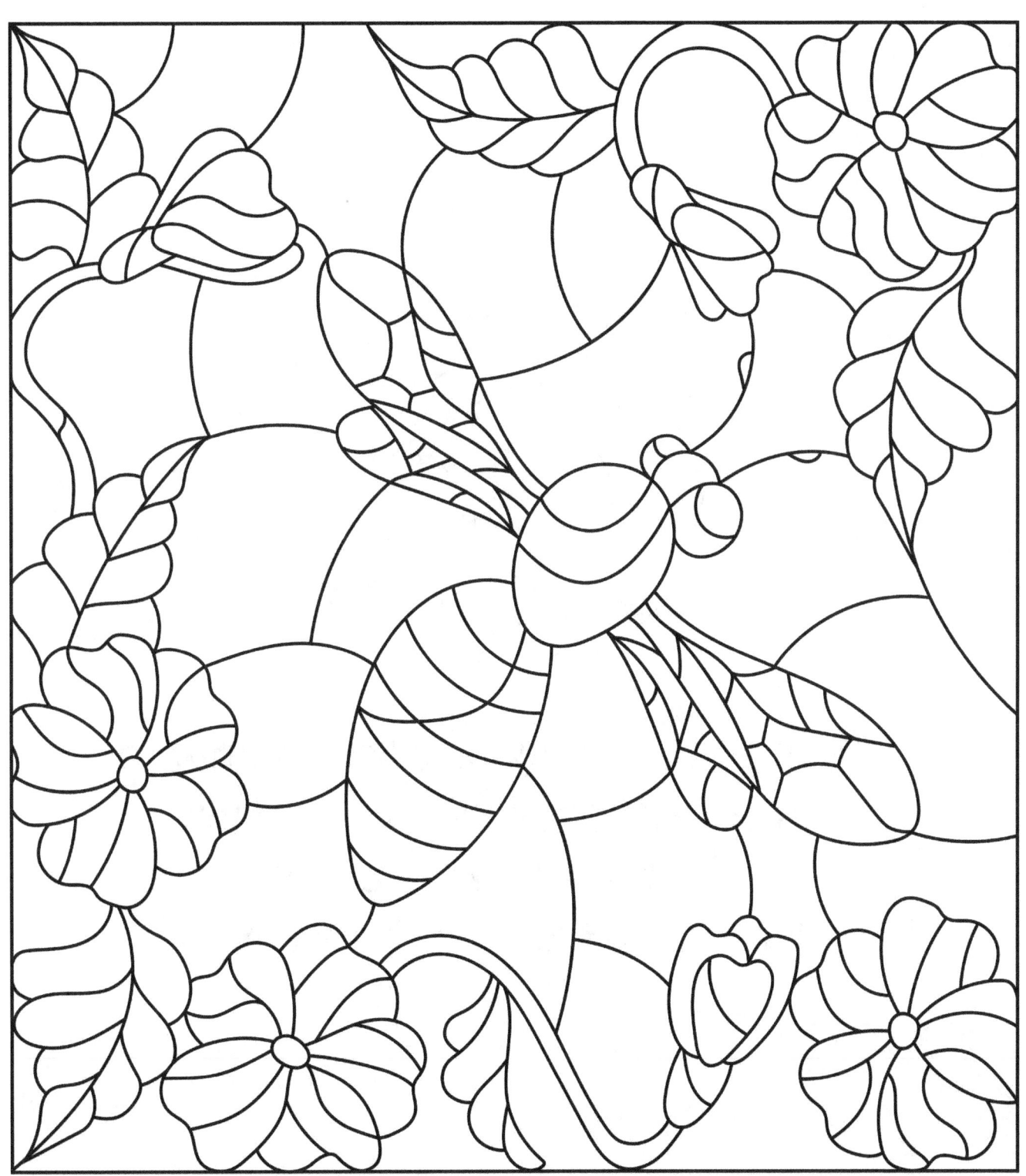

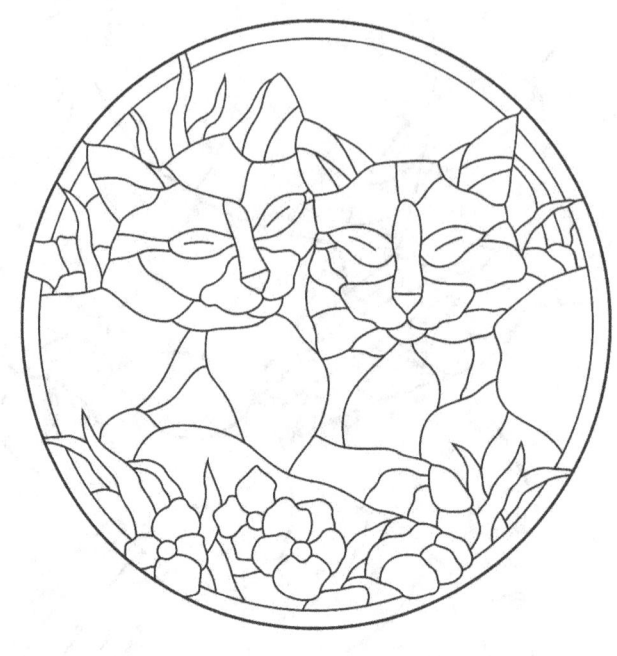

"For me a stained glass window
is a transparent partition
between my heart
and the heart of the world"

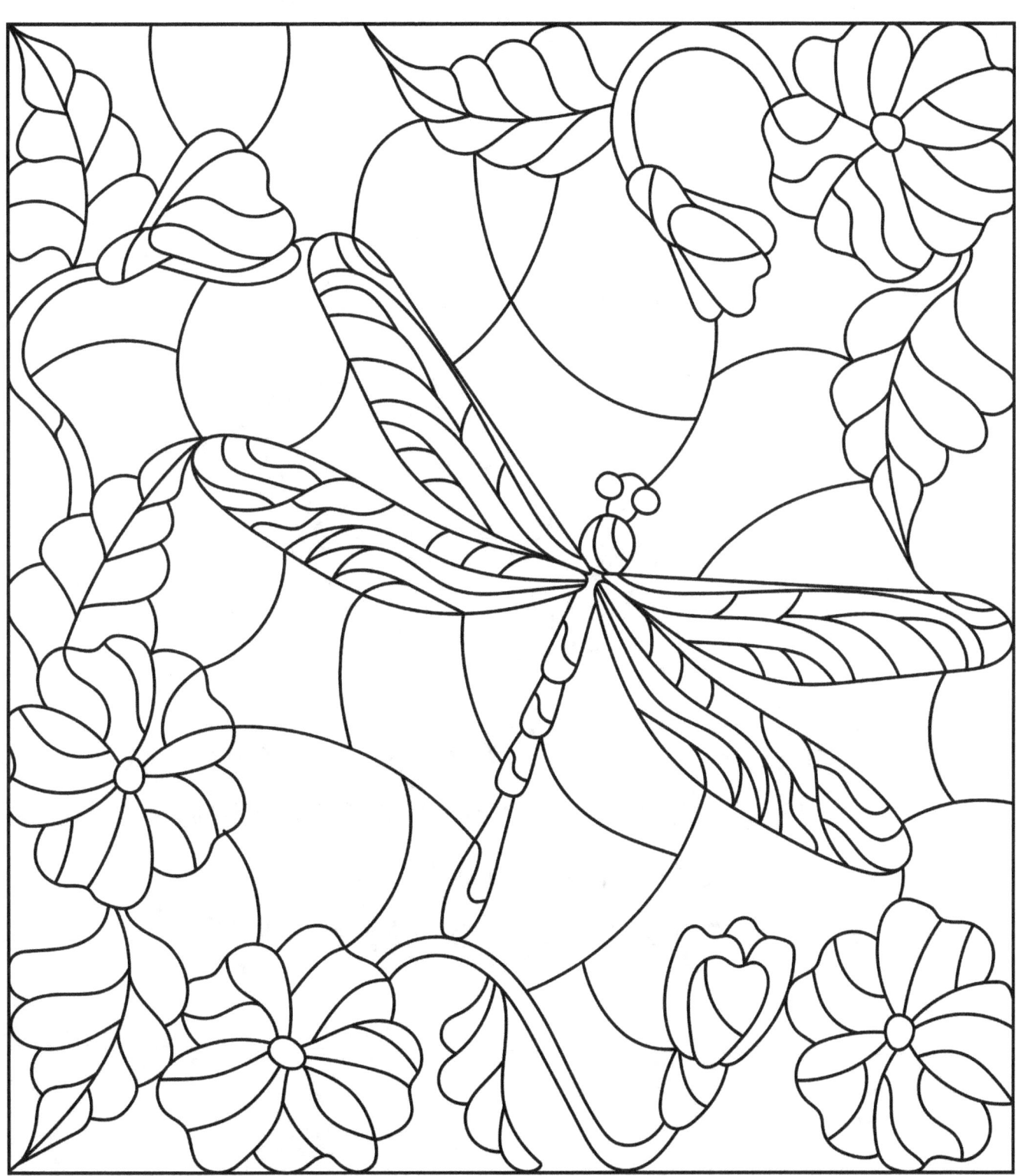

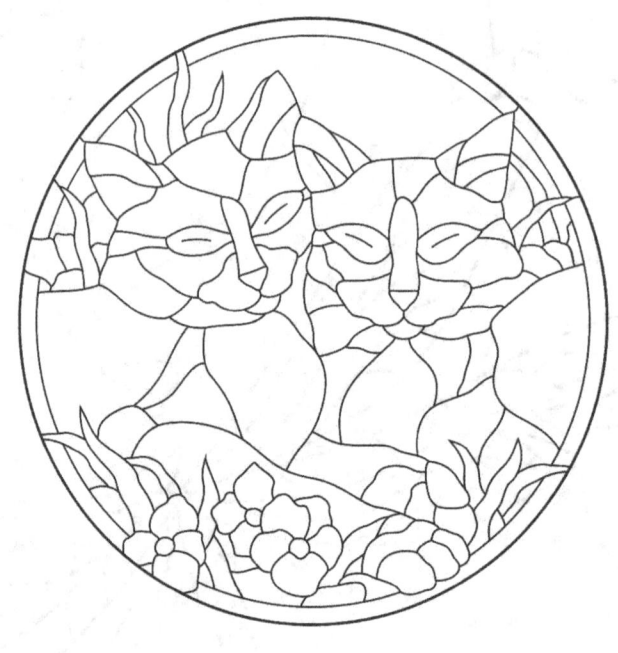

"For me a stained glass window
is a transparent partition
between my heart
and the heart of the world"

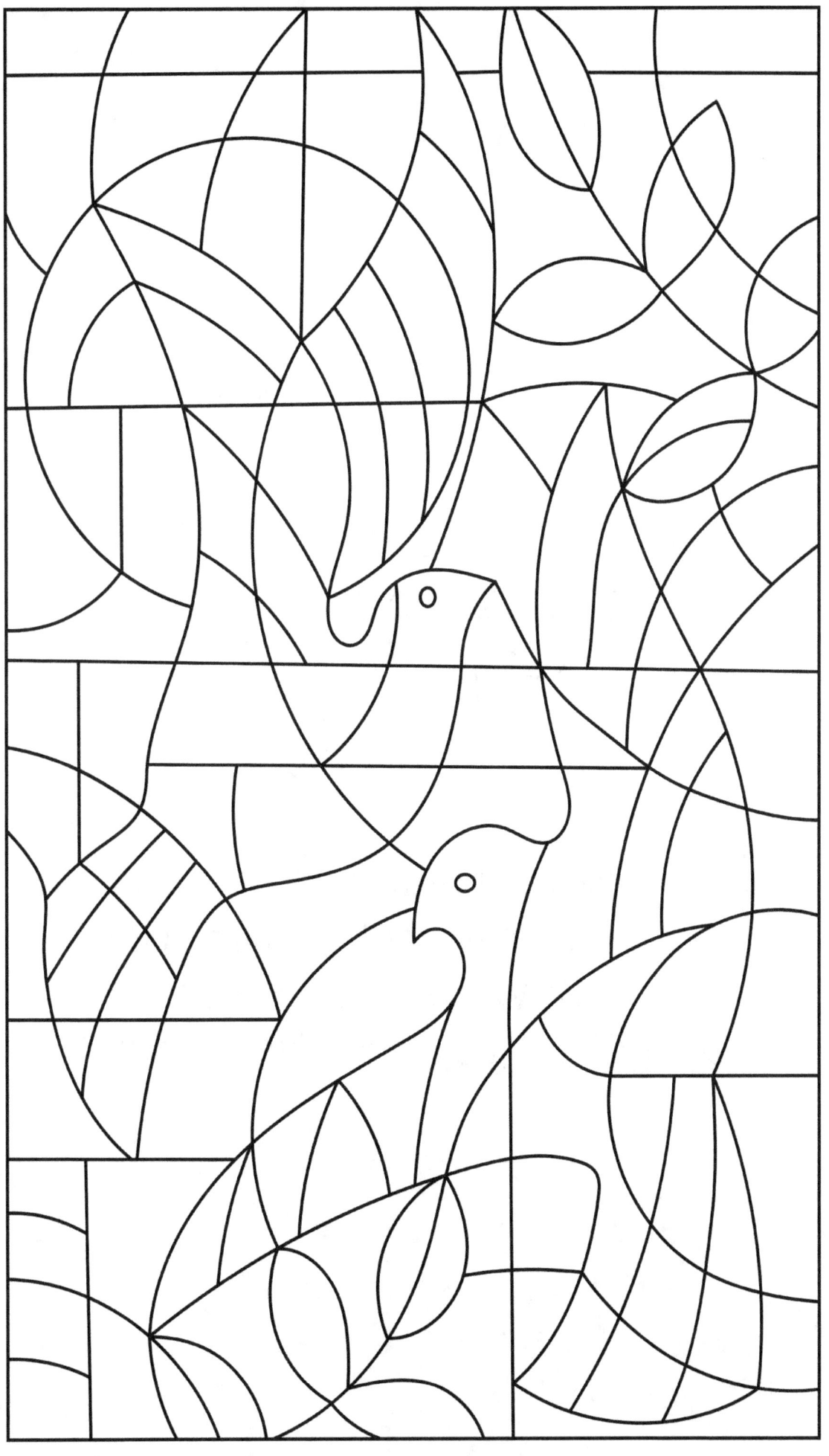

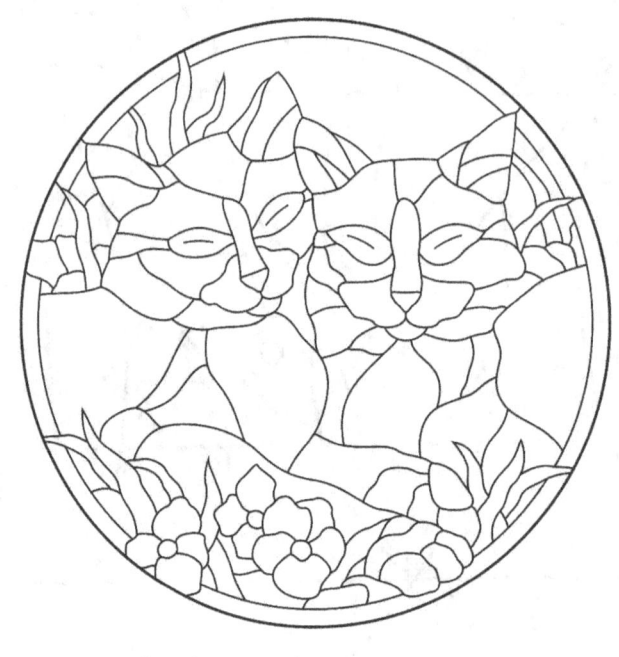

"For me a stained glass window
is a transparent partition
between my heart
and the heart of the world"

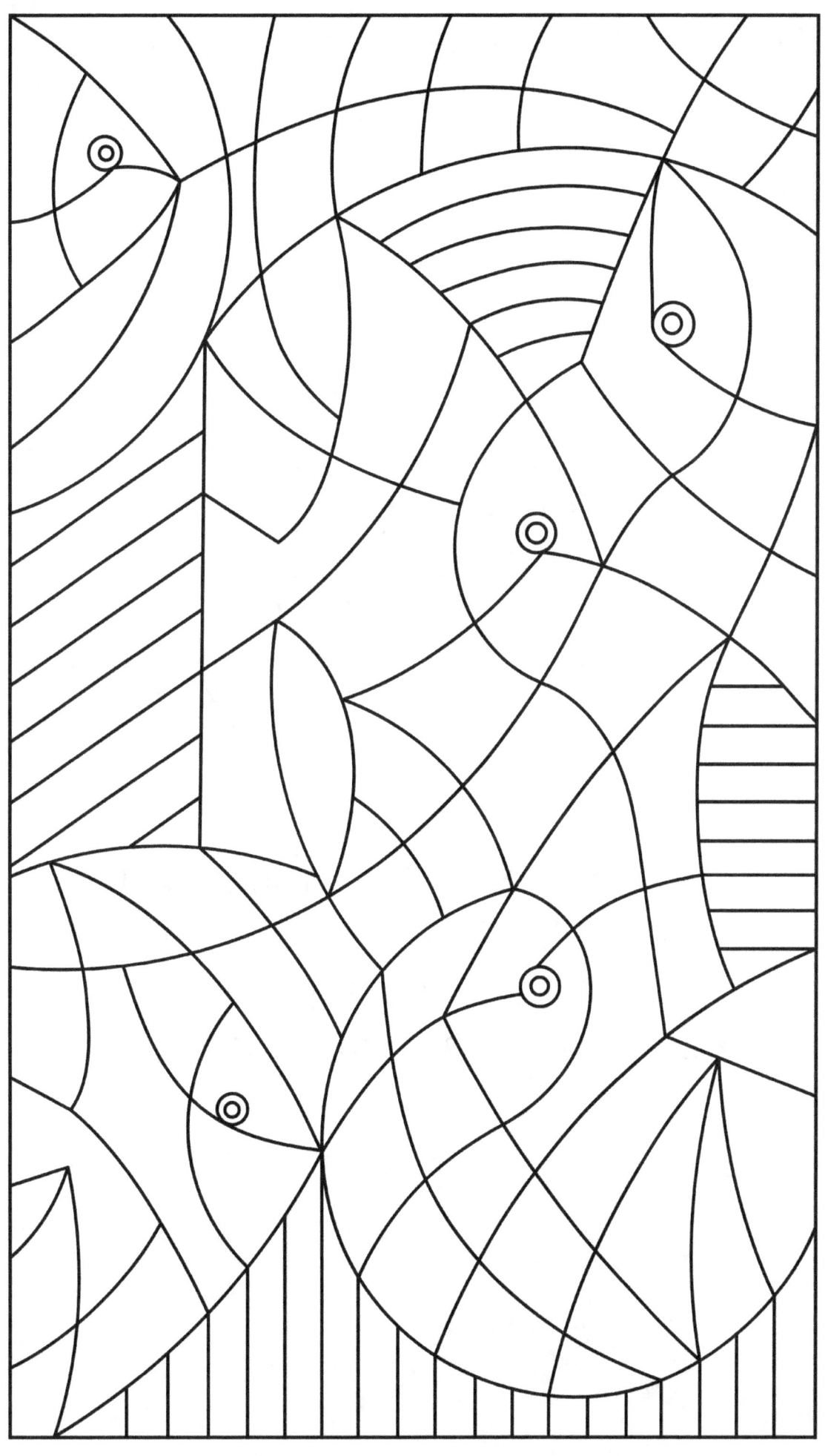

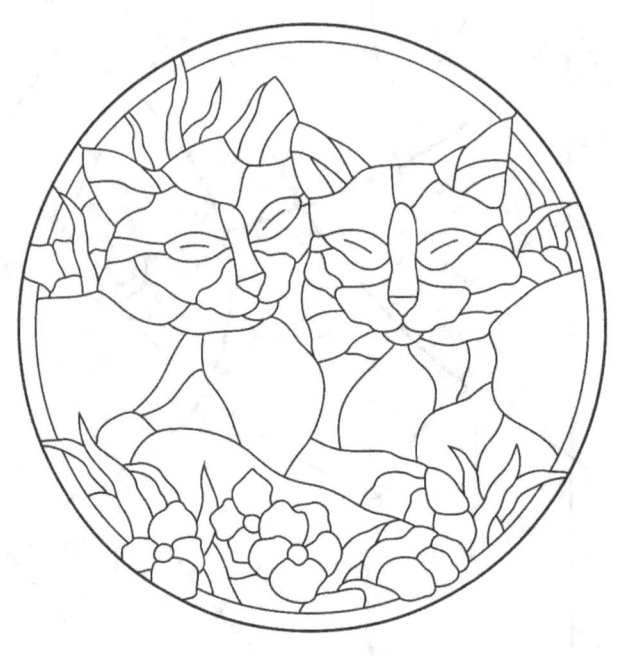

"For me a stained glass window
is a transparent partition
between my heart
and the heart of the world"

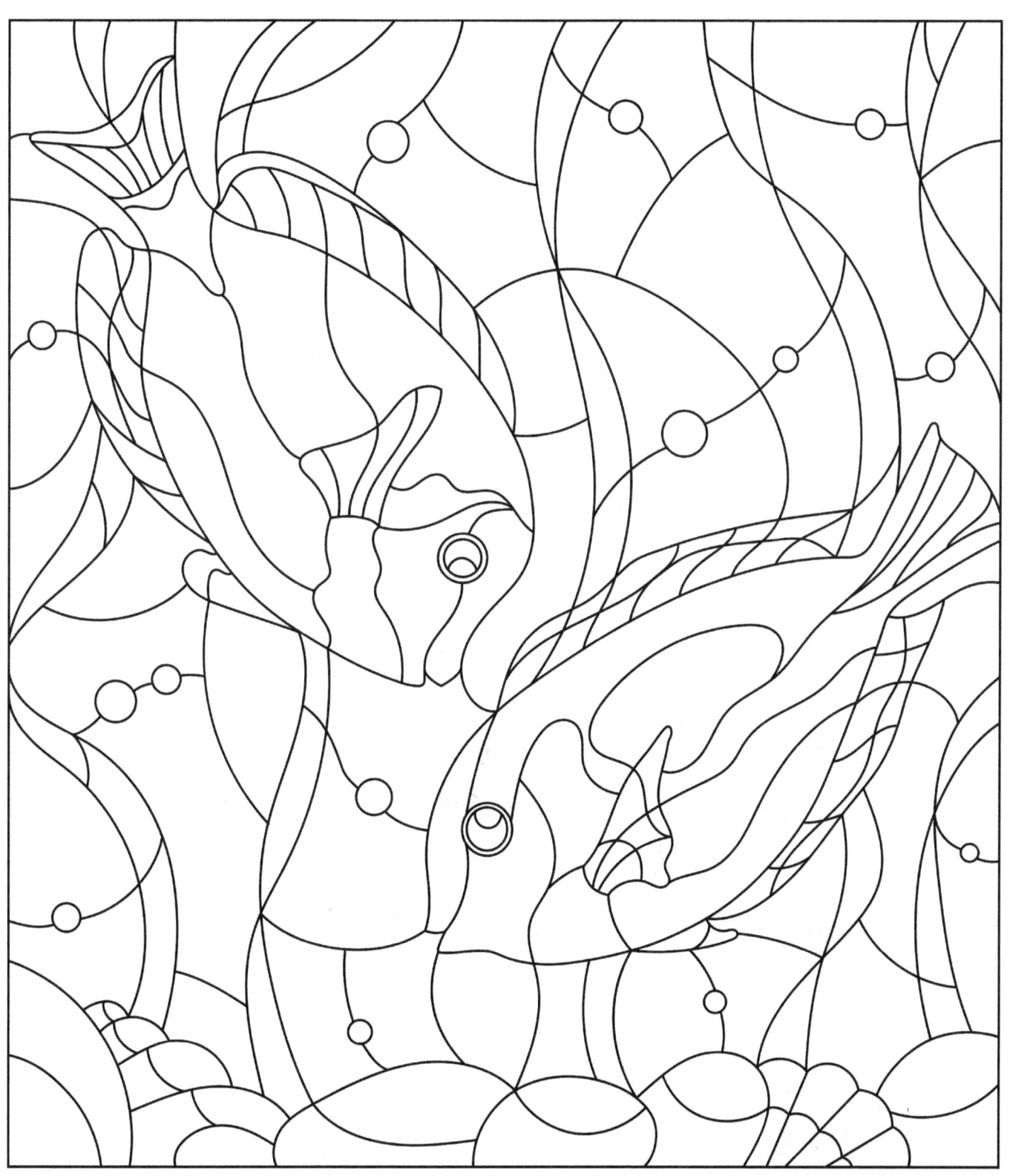

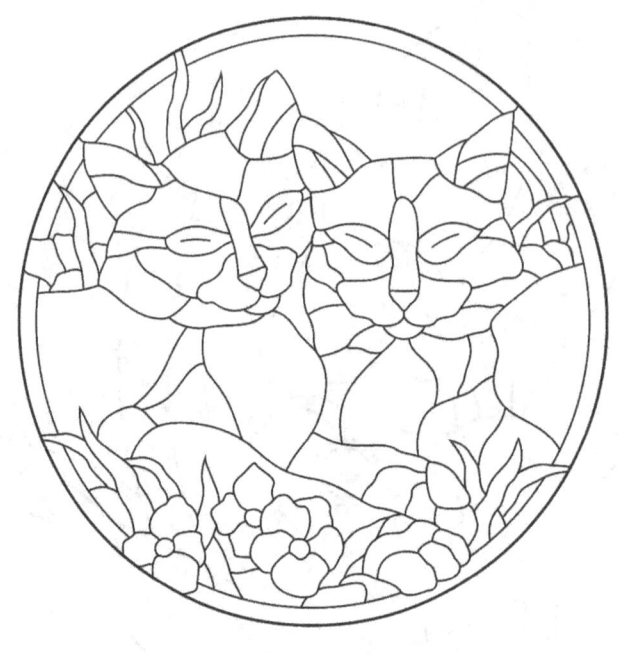

"For me a stained glass window
is a transparent partition
between my heart
and the heart of the world"

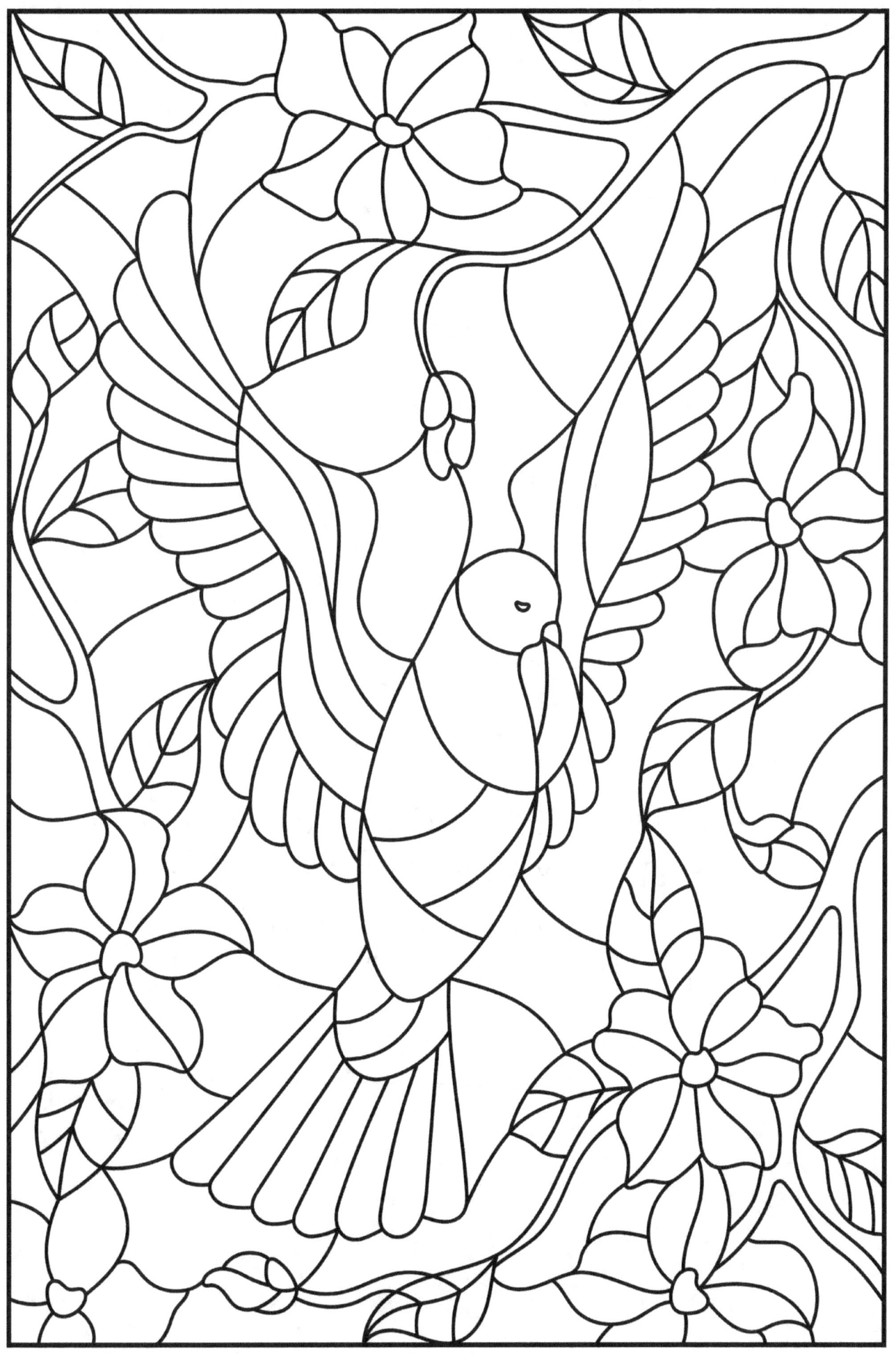

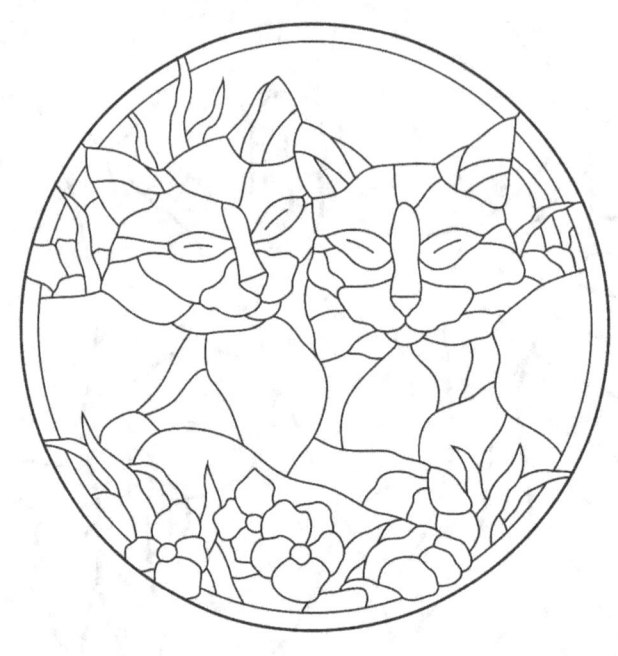

"For me a stained glass window
is a transparent partition
between my heart
and the heart of the world"

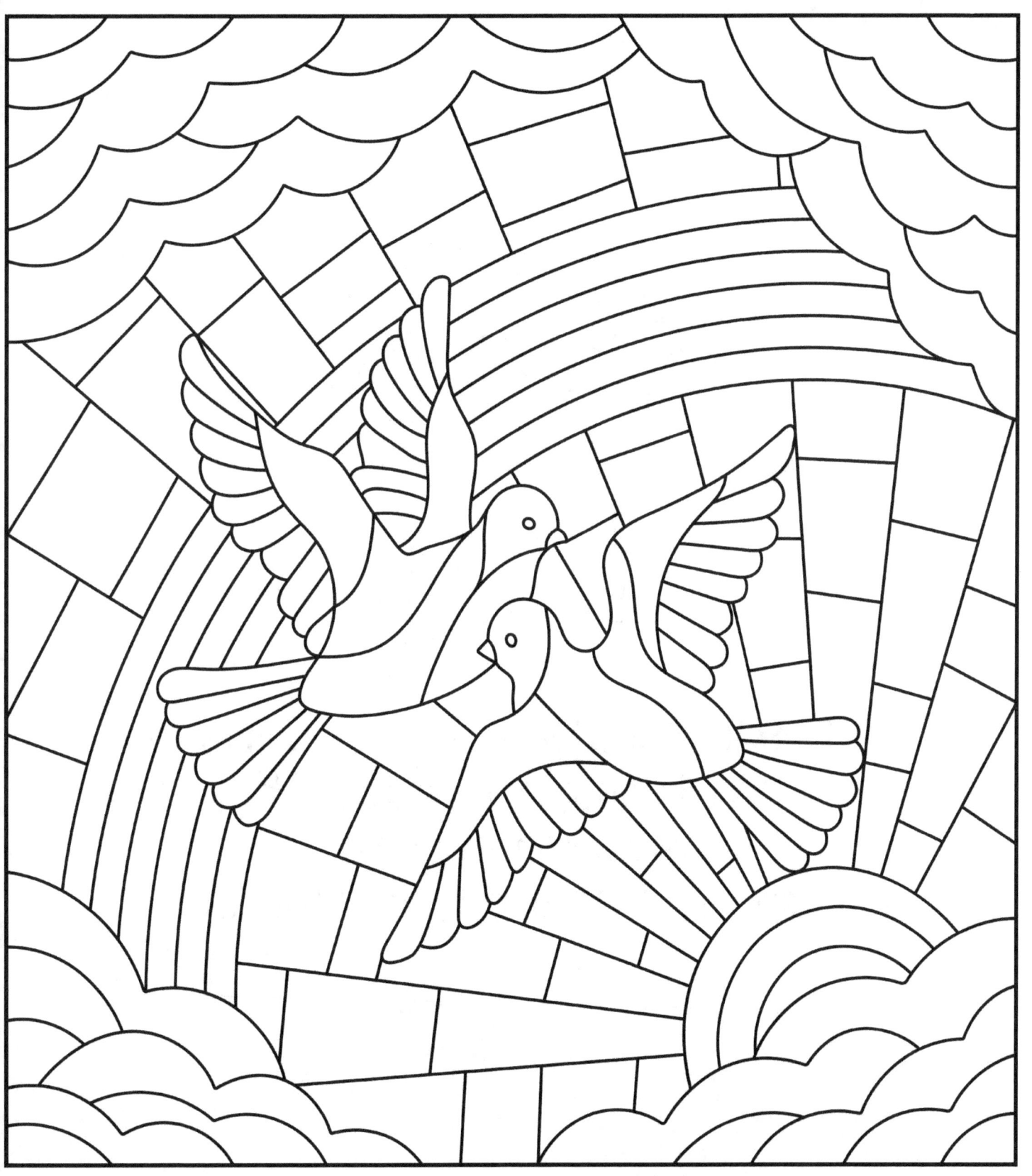

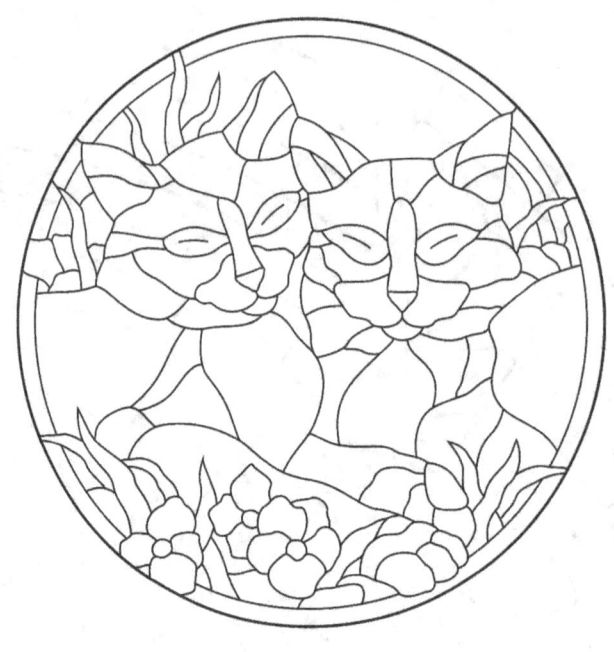

"For me a stained glass window
is a transparent partition
between my heart
and the heart of the world"

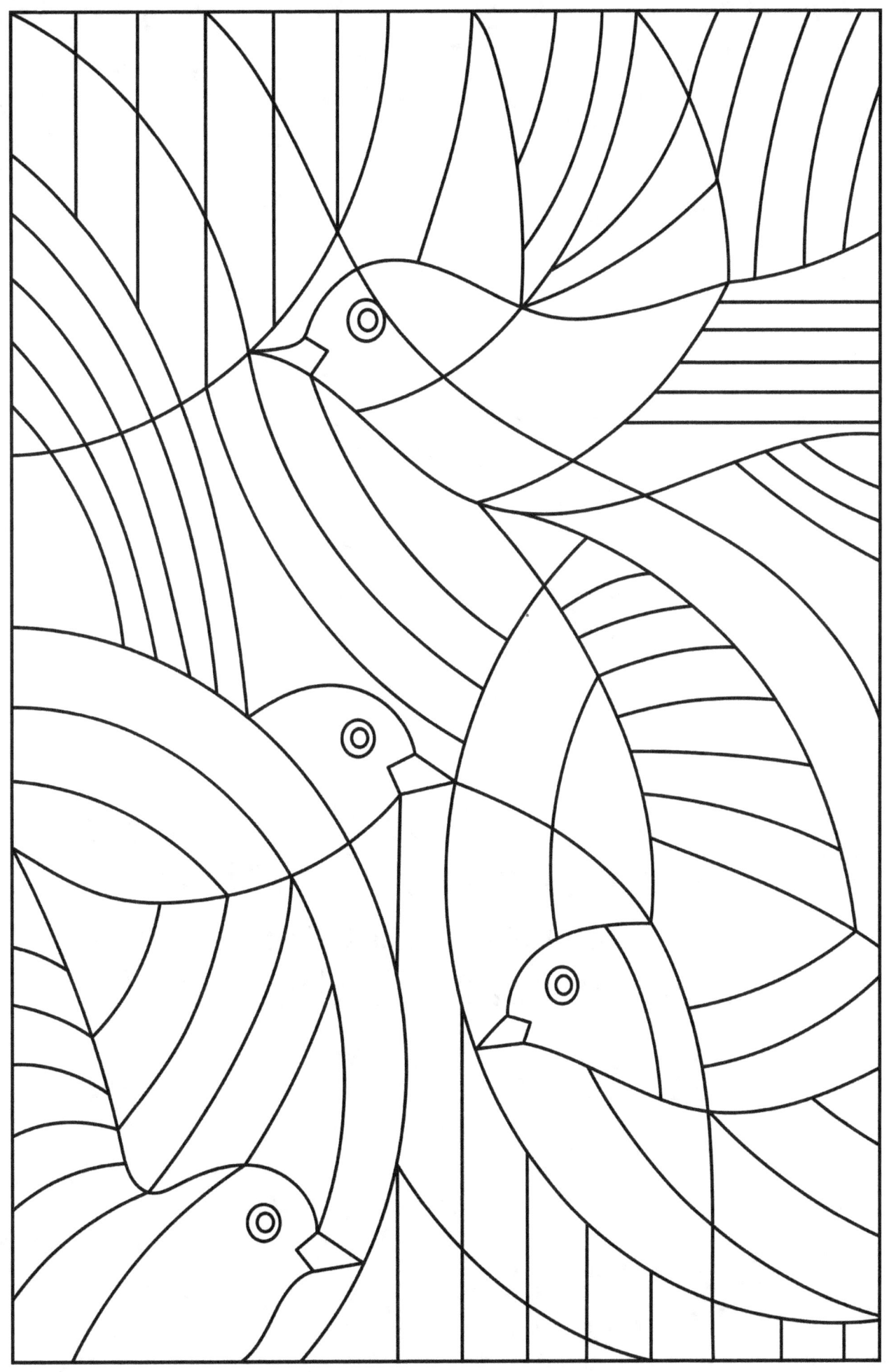

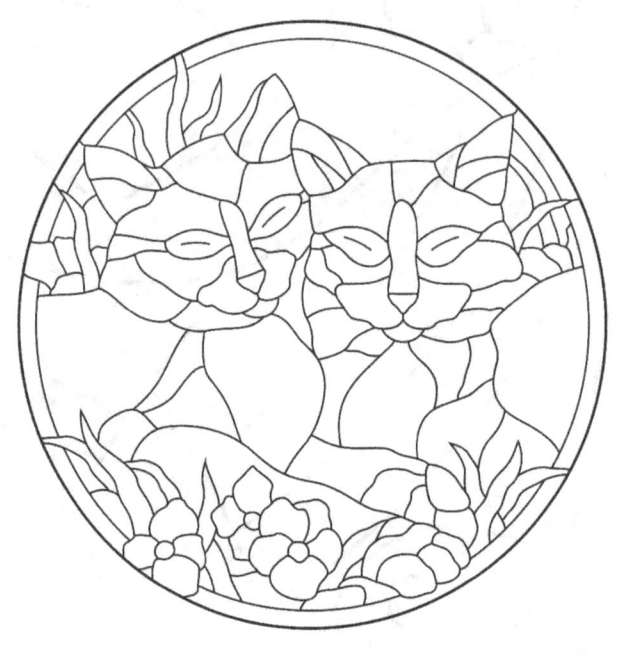

"For me a stained glass window
is a transparent partition
between my heart
and the heart of the world"

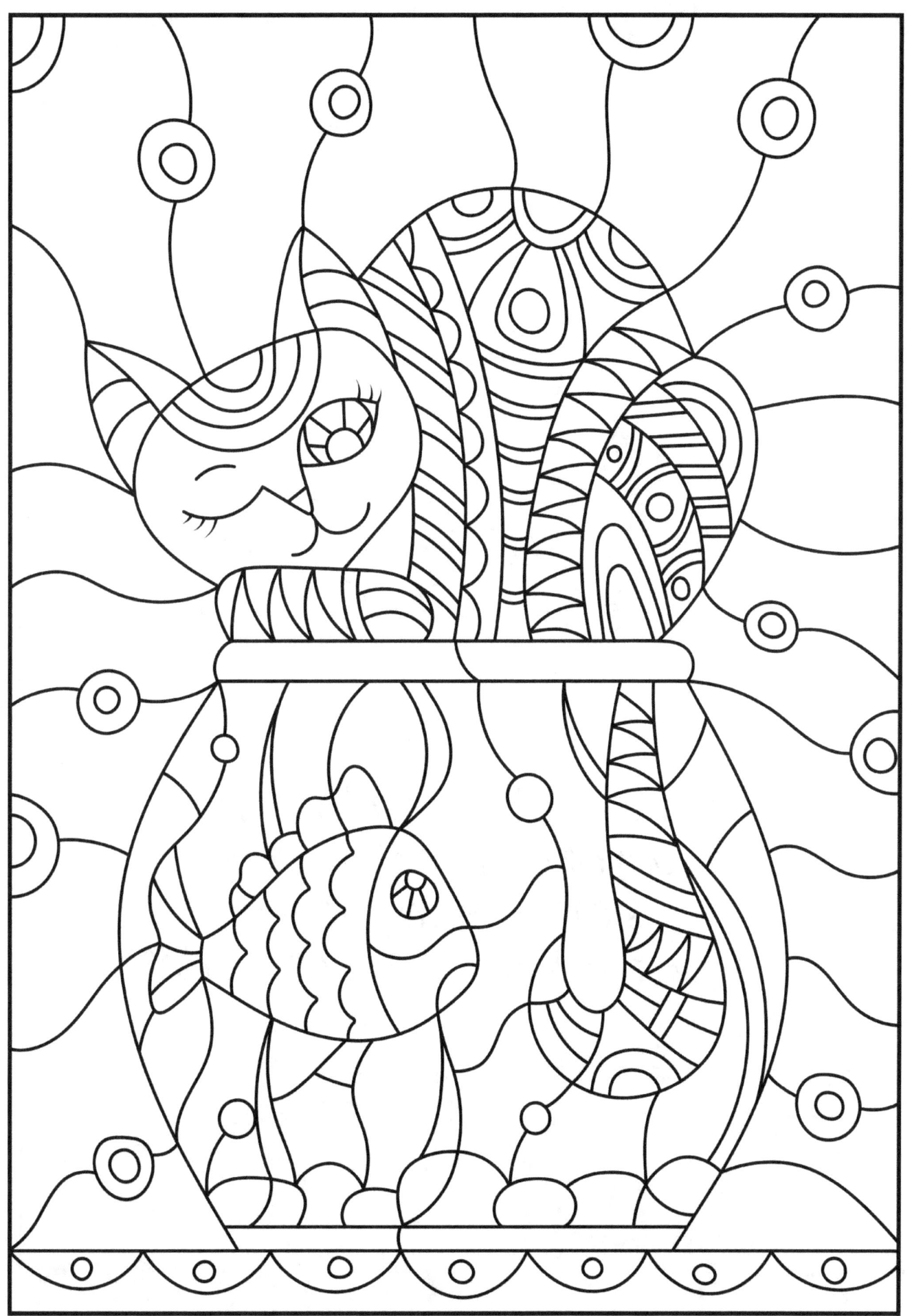

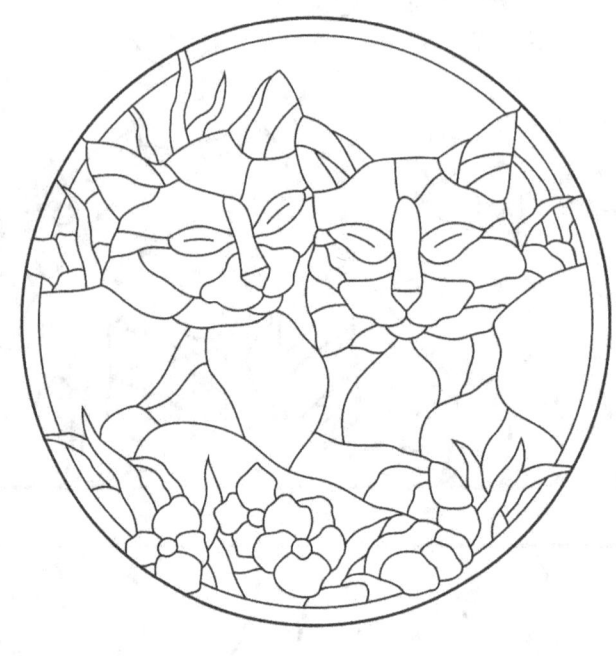

"For me a stained glass window
is a transparent partition
between my heart
and the heart of the world"

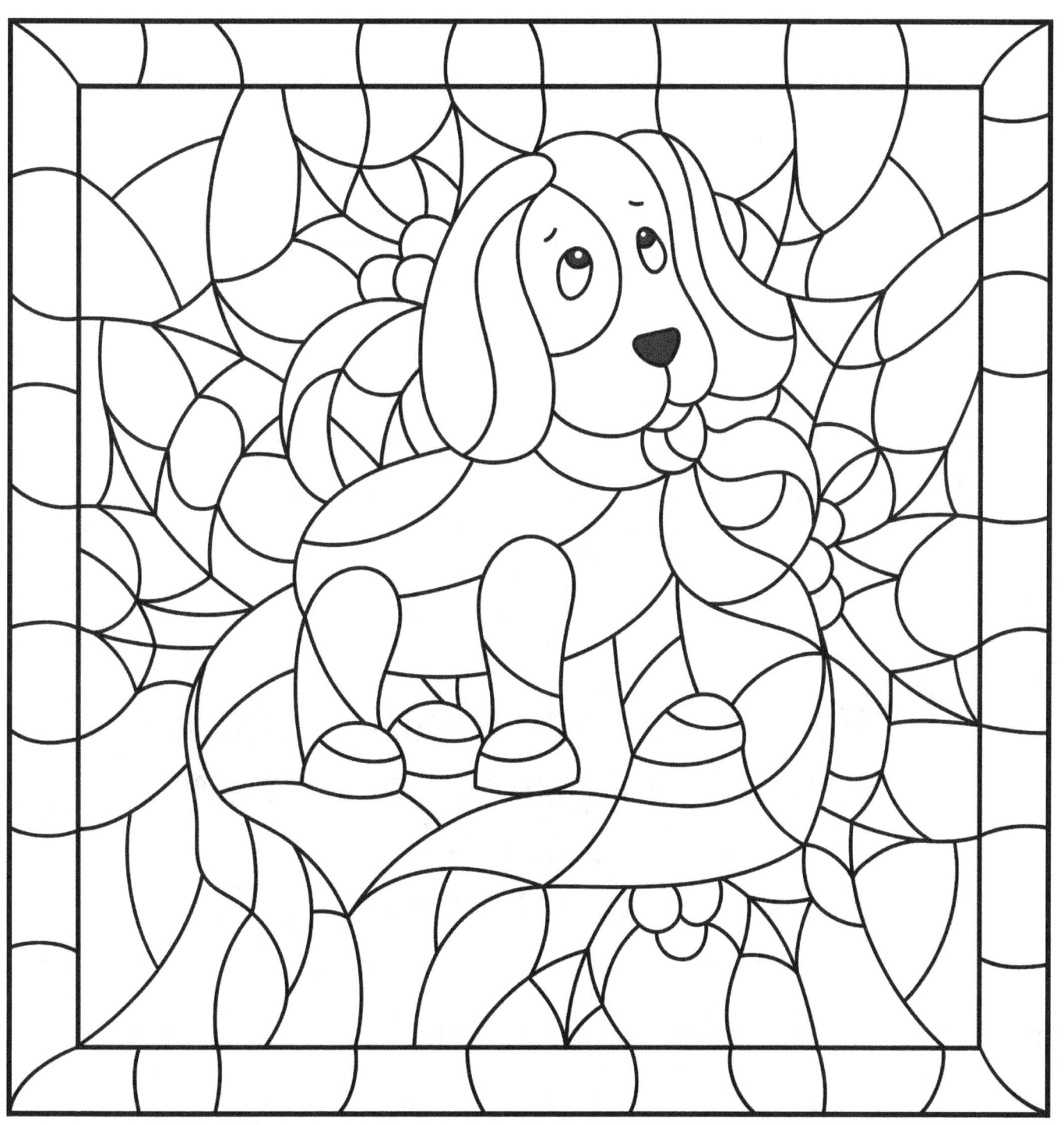

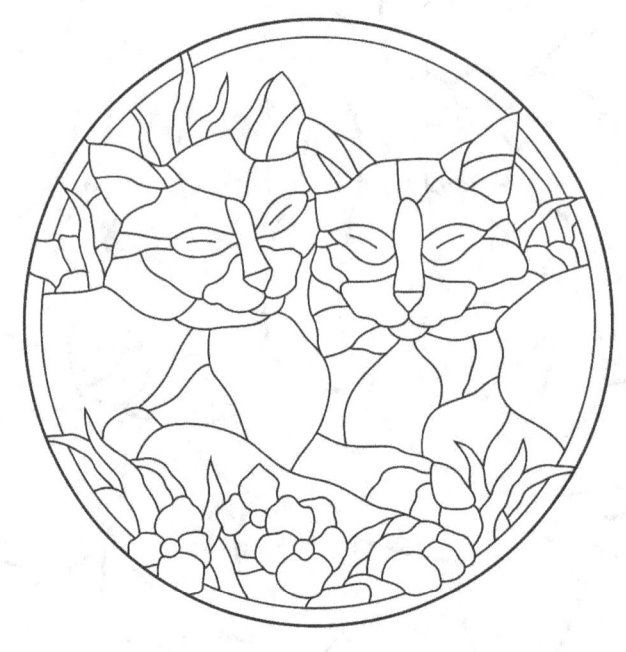

"For me a stained glass window
is a transparent partition
between my heart
and the heart of the world"

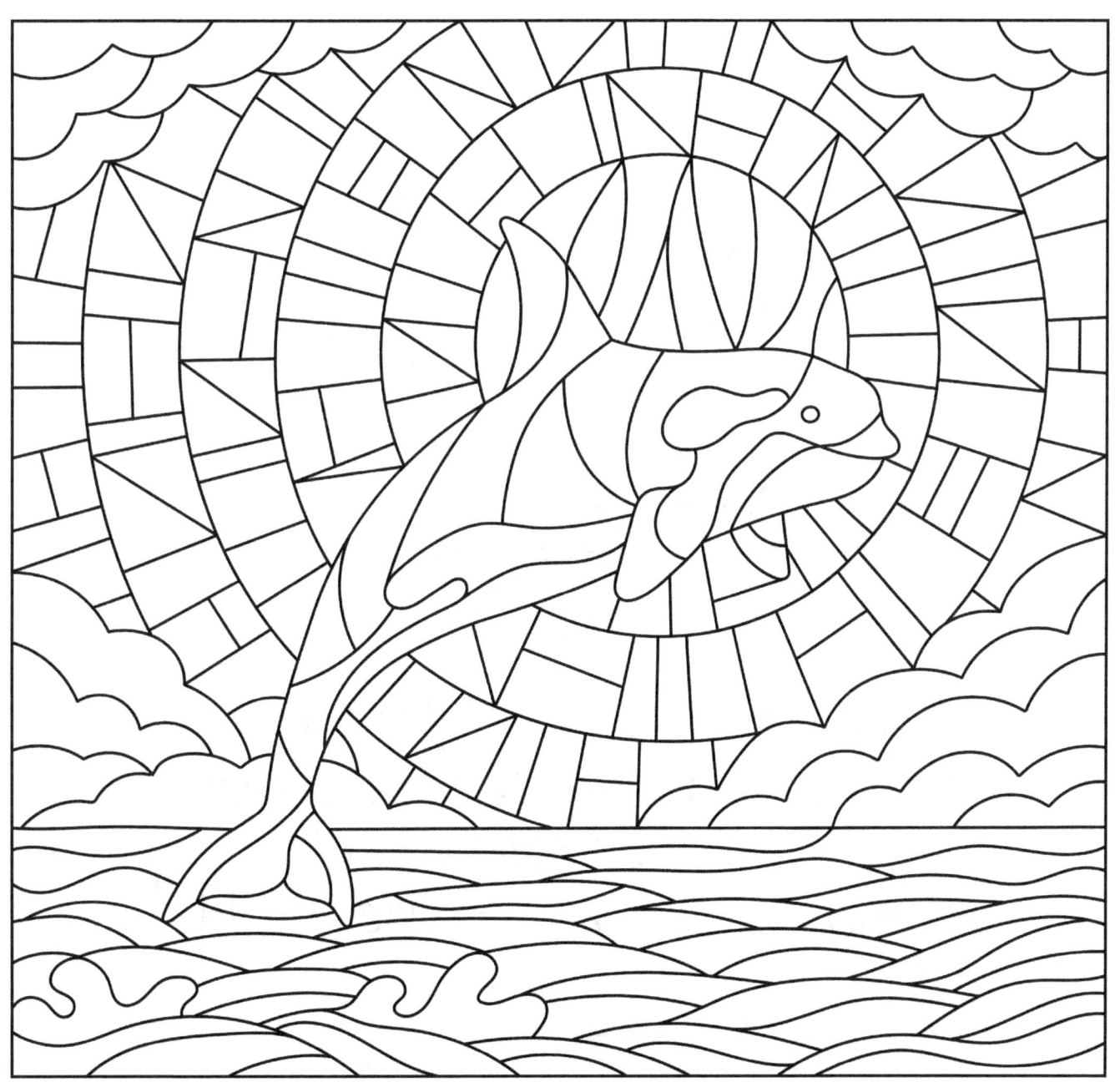

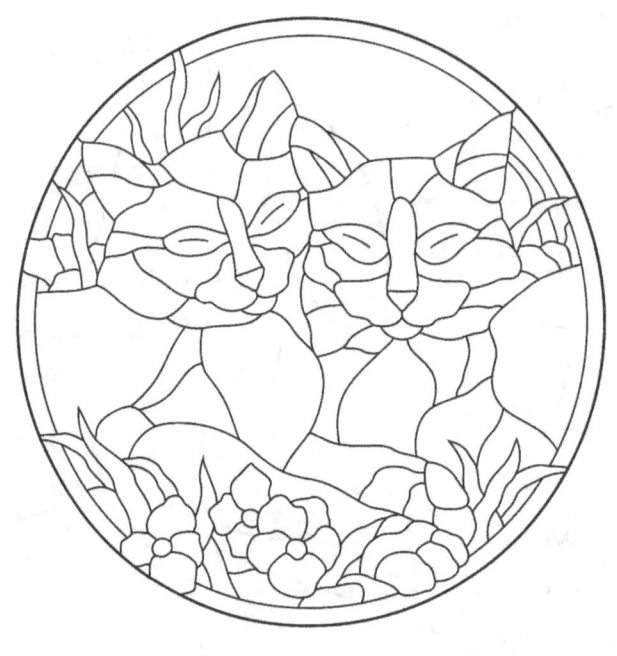

"For me a stained glass window
is a transparent partition
between my heart
and the heart of the world"

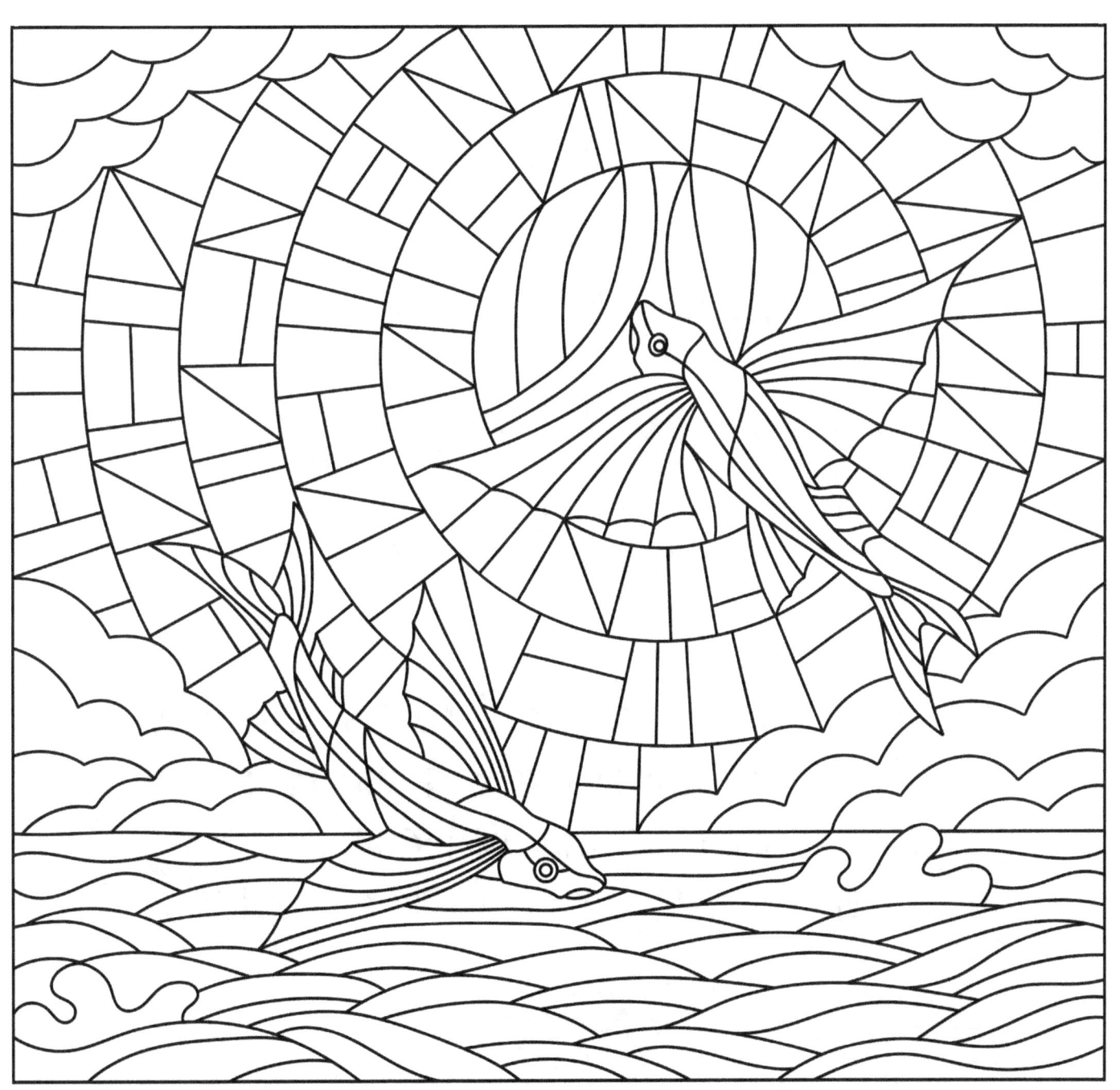

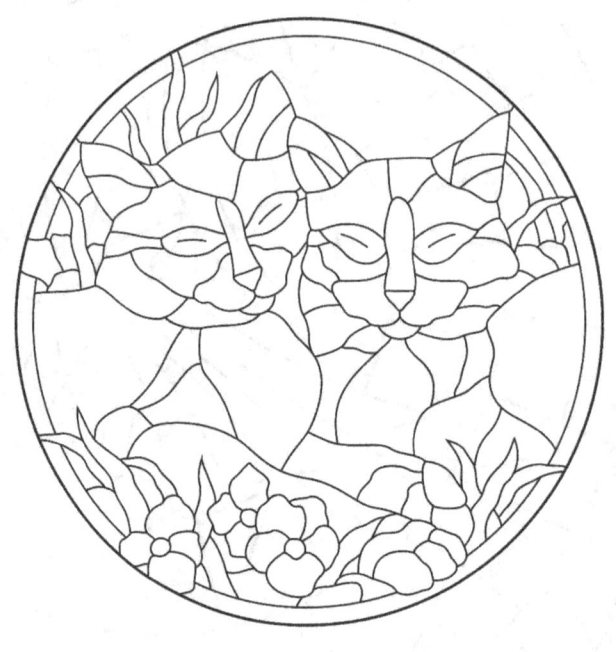

"For me a stained glass window
is a transparent partition
between my heart
and the heart of the world"

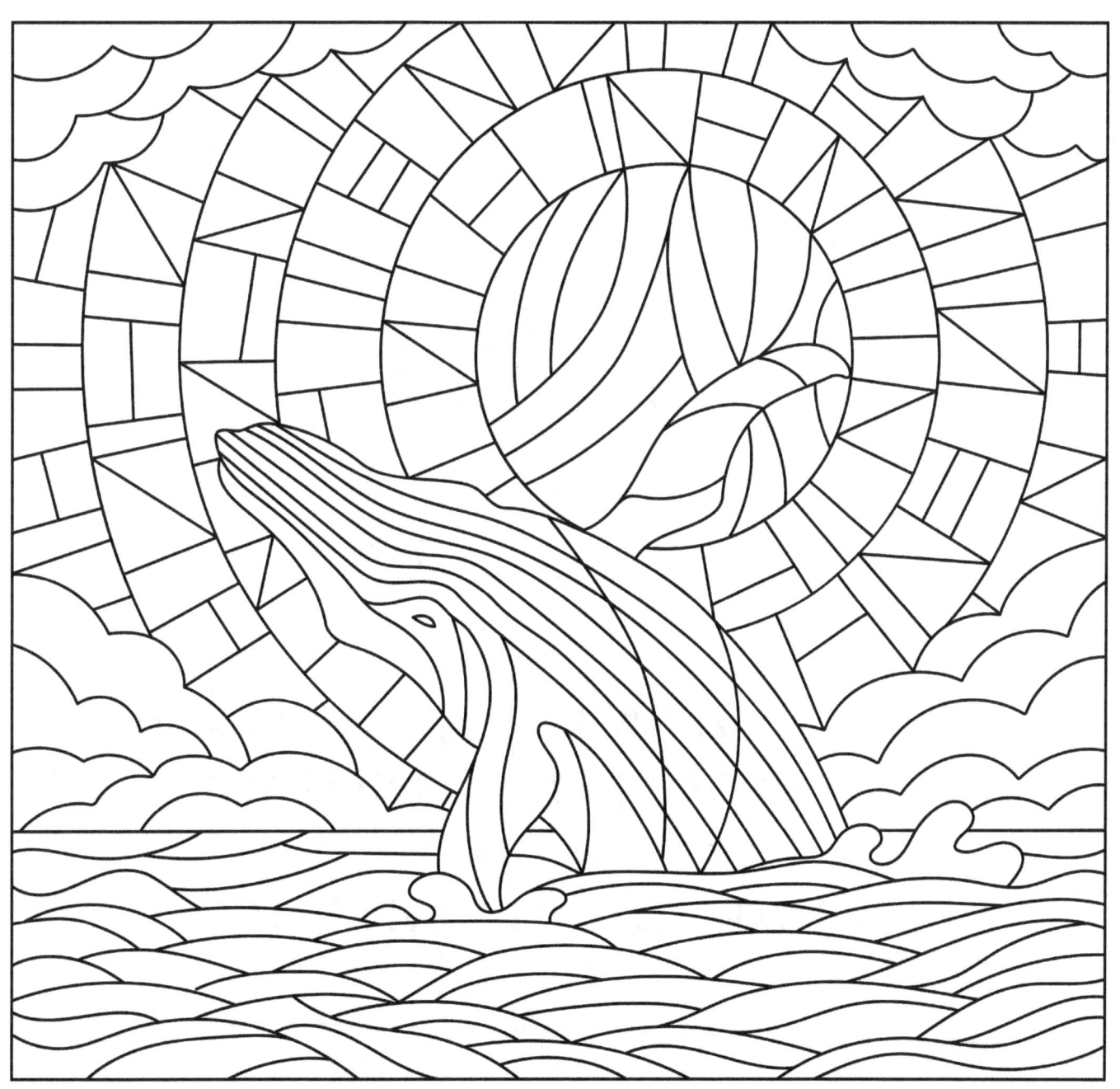

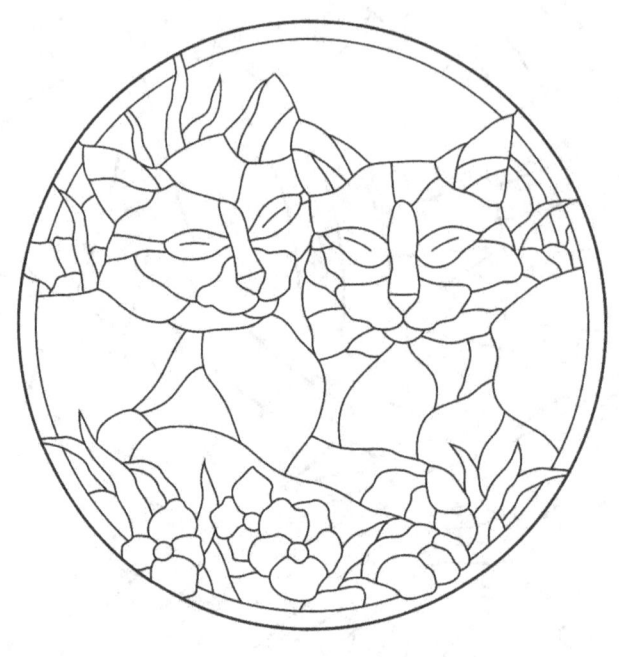

"For me a stained glass window
is a transparent partition
between my heart
and the heart of the world"

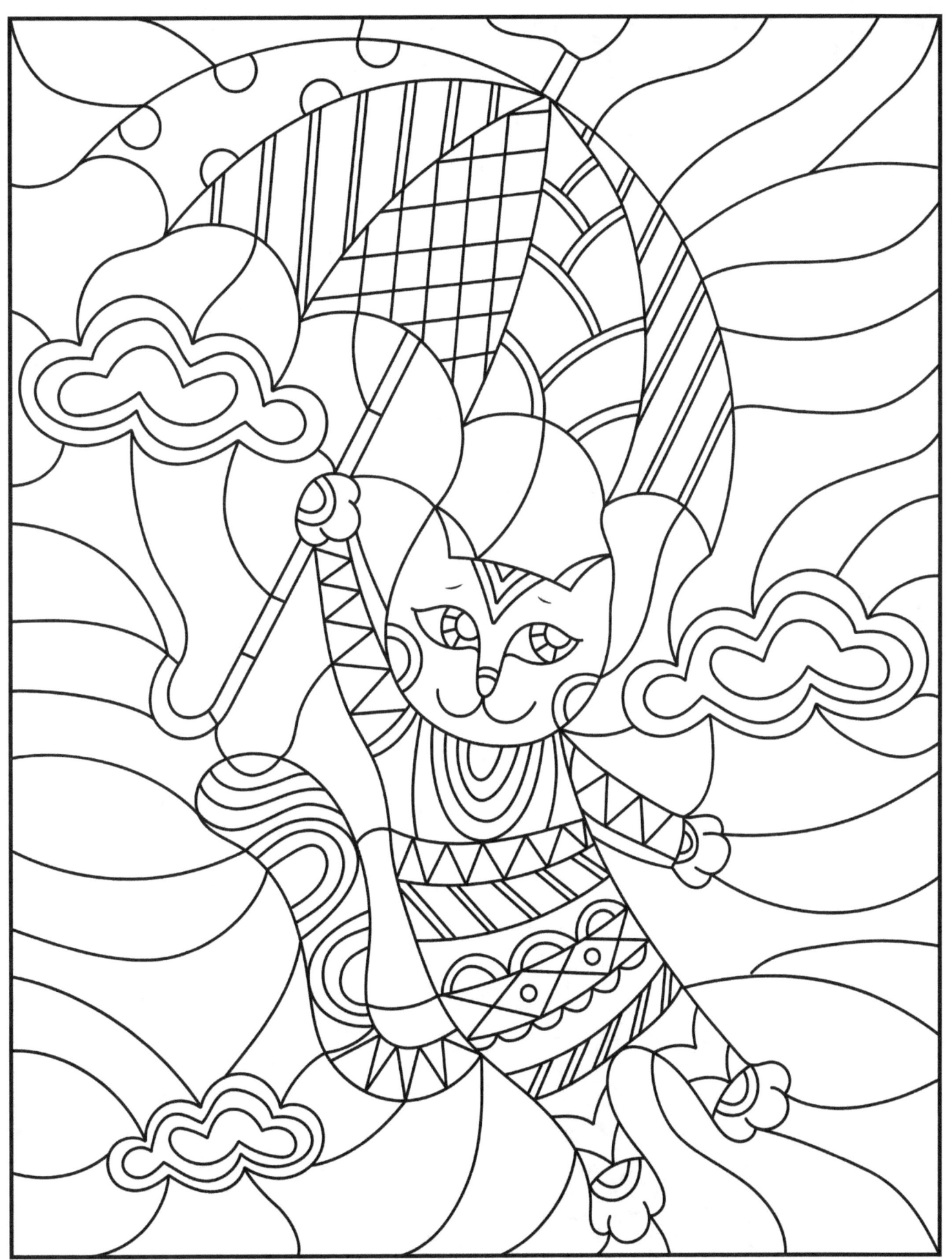

www.ingramcontent.com/pod-product-compliance
Lightning Source LLC
Chambersburg PA
CBHW080906220526

45466CB00011BA/3485